Richmond
First
Certificate
Practice Tests

Diana L Fried-Booth

Contents

Introduction

This book contains five Practice Tests for the Cambridge First Certificate in English examination. The tests reflect the kind of materials and tasks you can expect to come across when you take the FCE itself. They have been taken from a wide range of authentic sources and also reflect the topic areas which form the basis of the examination.

During your English lessons your teacher will have been preparing you for the FCE examination by using a course book. These five tests should be used for practice purposes in the few weeks before you take the exam. In this way the tests will give you practice not only in coping with the kinds of tasks you will be required to complete in the exam, but also with the amount of time allowed for each paper. By the time you reach the fifth and last Practice Test, you should feel confident about your ability to work quickly and accurately within the time limit for each paper.

Always make sure that you have checked through and corrected each test before proceeding to the next test and that you have discussed with your teacher any particular difficulties. In this way you should be able to focus on any problems which need your teacher's help.

Results

You can take the examination twice a year: in June and December.

There are three pass grades: A, B, C; and three fail grades: D, E, and U. A minimum grade C pass corresponds to approximately 60% of the total mark.

When you get your results, you will be notified if you have done particularly well or badly on individual papers.

You can take the examination twice a year: in June and December.

Exam structure

Each test contains the five papers which comprise the complete FCE examination: Reading, Writing, Use of English, Listening and Speaking. You are advised to tackle Papers 1, 2 and 3 in the order in which you will take them in the exam itself. Papers 4 and 5 need not be done on the same day.

Each paper is worth 40 marks, and the marks for the individual papers are added together to form a total mark out of 200. The raw scores for each paper are scaled so that each paper receives equal weighting.

EACH PAPER COMPRISES THE FOLLOWING SECTIONS:

PAPER 1

Reading
1 hour 15 minutes
35 questions

PAPER 2

Writing
1 hour 30 minutes
2 writing tasks

PAPER 3

Use of English
1 hour 15 minutes
65 questions

PAPER 4

Listening
Approximately 40 minutes
30 questions

PAPER 5

Speaking
14 minutes
Paired interview in 4 parts

For further information about the FCE, write to:

UCLES
1 Hills Road
Cambridge
CB1 2EU
UK

Practice Test 1

PAPER 1   Reading

PART 1

You are going to read a newspaper article about students who sail the world studying as they go. Choose the most suitable heading from the list **A-I** for each part **(1-7)** of the article. There is one extra heading which you do not need to use. There is an example at the beginning **(0)**.

Mark your answers **on the separate answer sheet**.

A	The regular routine
B	What students learn about
C	Popular routes already sailed
D	Applicant's ideal background
E	Encouraging teamwork skills
F	The organisation's philosophy
G	When the voyages started
H	The need to obey regulations
I	The effects of the voyage

A swell way to learn

0   **G**

In 1985 a foundation called *Class Afloat*, based in Quebec, Canada, organised a voyage for about fifty students aged 16 to 18. However, this was no ordinary holiday voyage but an opportunity for students to study as they sailed, and over the years the voyages have become increasingly popular.

1

The ten-month-long trips are open to any student who can afford the cost of about $25,000 which includes trips on land when the ship is in port and the purchase of any necessary textbooks. The organisers look for candidates who have a good academic record and an ability to get on with others. You must be fit and healthy but you don't need to have sailed before.

2

The ship is manned by a professional crew and a separate teaching staff. One of the ship's directors says that students return dramatically different from when they joined. 'By the end they are much more responsible individuals. Their eyes and minds are opened so much that they can't help but grow up.'

3

A typical day at sea includes six hours in the classroom studying a range of subjects, all of which are taught in English. In addition, two hours are spent on various duties on the ship, two hours more on the deck overnight, and one hour a day on physical training and nautical science.

4

Class Afloat believe in taking the classroom to the world. Students study cultures by being there, not through reading textbooks or listening to someone else who's been there. Students have the experience of seeing different cultures and, on a personal level, become more mature and more tolerant.

5

Anthropology, maths, chemistry, economics, social studies, history and geography are among the subjects taught. In bad weather students will be amused by the sight of the teacher falling over while trying hard to maintain the attention of the class. Air-conditioning on board, however, makes life easier.

6

On-board behaviour is governed by a set of strict rules. Students must sign an agreement to keep the rules, and anyone who breaks these rules risks being punished or worst of all forbidden to continue the voyage. Smoking is allowed in only one place on deck, and never below. In port, students are allowed out only in groups of four, never singly, for reasons of safety.

7

Slowly but surely as the students get to know each other, they develop a crew spirit. Each person is essential to the trip and the ship can't reach the next port without every member of the crew. Inevitably, the limits of life at sea mean that relationships often develop. And while there is no rule against relationships on the trip, boys and girls are not allowed into cabins belonging to the opposite sex.

PART 2

You are going to read an extract from an interview with a musician. For Questions **8-15**, choose the answer **(A, B, C** or **D)** which you think fits best according to the text.

Mark your answers **on the separate answer sheet**.

There is nothing to suggest that Evelyn Glennie is profoundly deaf. She insists that her deafness is irrelevant to her musicianship, but there is no doubt that her obvious handicap has turned a remarkable career into a miraculous one.

line 4

She was eight when her hearing began to fail; by twelve she had lost it completely and feared she would have to give up the music she loved. But a doctor's suggestion that she should become an accountant rather than follow a hopeless musical career strengthened her will to succeed.

She grew up on a farm in Scotland. From an early age her great love was the piano, and after enjoying the audience applause at a prize-winning performance she decided on a career as a soloist. By then, however, her love of the piano had been overtaken by her passion for playing percussion instruments like the drums, an almost impossible task for a deaf person. 'You need to be very sensitive because you are dealing with literally thousands of instruments,' she says. 'Anyone can strike something and get a sound but you have to learn to control it and that can take a lifetime's work.'

line 23

As it turned out, music was one of the most advantageous careers she could have chosen and is one reason why her speech remains so extraordinarily correct, despite her deafness. 'You can relate a lot of what you feel through the instruments onto your own voice box, so you know how to pitch, how to adjust your voice,' she says.

Occasionally she listens to recordings by holding a cassette player between her knees, interpreting the vibrations and the shaking movements. Her deafness is one of the reasons for her unique style, for she can't listen and be influenced by other performances and she has often declared that getting her hearing back would be the worst thing that could happen to her. 'It would be like giving sight to a blind person who had fitted their life to what they saw through their hands. Quite apart from that, I am so critical of what I do anyway that I wouldn't want to be comparing myself to others.'

As a result of her devotion to her music and her determination to succeed, she has doubled the range of works available for percussion music in Europe and introduced instruments previously unheard of in the west. She has also asked composers to write more than fifty new pieces of music for these instruments, and has set up a library of three hundred works for other musicians to use.

8   What do you think the phrase 'obvious handicap' (line 4) means in this context?
    A   an emotional disadvantage
    B   a physical achievement
    C   a clear musical advantage
    D   an apparent physical disability

9   What added to Glennie's determination not to give up on a musical career?
    A   her doctor's advice
    B   her love of the piano
    C   her dislike of accountancy
    D   her success in a competition

10   Why did Glennie want to be a solo performer?
    A   Not many people played the drums.
    B   It was easier if you were deaf.
    C   She liked praise and attention.
    D   She knew she was a good pianist.

11   What does 'it' in line 23 refer to?
    A   being sensitive to reactions to deafness
    B   a lifetime's work in the world of orchestral music
    C   being in technical command of an instrument
    D   finding time to learn many different instruments

12   Why was music such a good choice of career?
    A   It enables her to speak well.
    B   It has made her voice softer.
    C   It helps with her deafness.
    D   It has made her famous.

13   Glennie thinks that being deaf is an advantage because it means her
    A   audience is sympathetic.
    B   interpretation is her own.
    C   style is better than others.
    D   performance is influential.

14   Why does Glennie dislike the idea of comparison with others?
    A   She is too critical of other people.
    B   She criticises herself already.
    C   She is afraid of harsh criticism.
    D   She thinks her critics are unfair.

15   What would be the most suitable title for this extract?
    A   How to be a successful musician
    B   The disadvantages of deafness
    C   Developing one's musical skills
    D   Overcoming a severe disability

PART 3

You are going to read a newspaper article about students who take a year off after leaving university, before looking for a job. Eight sentences have been removed from the article. Choose from the sentences **A-I** the one which fits each gap **(16-22)**. There is one extra sentence which you do not need to use. There is an example at the beginning **(0)**.

Mark your answers **on the separate answer sheet**.

A Indeed, students over 25 with the right qualities might be able to work as a leader on certain projects.

B It is surprising how cheap this type of holiday can be, and casual work is reasonably easy to find in some of the typical destinations.

C According to the marketing manager of Campus Travel, a travel agency which specialises in student travel, gap years may even make students more attractive to future employers.

D One advantage is that employers will often pay for the work that is done even if people are not fully qualified, so raising extra funds is not necessary.

E This is the choice which offers the greatest freedom and is by far the most popular.

F The first way is to join one of the expeditions or projects run by organisations or international charities.

G And now the 'gap year', which has traditionally attracted students who liked to travel between leaving school and going to university, is being taken seriously by employers and graduates alike.

H The opportunities for linking a student's future employment with a work placement scheme or industrial training are on the increase.

I As a result of this change, many travel agencies, including Campus Travel, have seen a huge increase in demand for round-the-world tickets in the last few years.

Just The Ticket

Travel requires time, money and a desire to see beyond the supermarket on the edge of town. Despite financial limits, students have always been great travellers, as the vacations offer opportunities for long-distance travel, expeditions or just doing very little on a faraway beach. **0** **G** Students in the last year of university are queuing up to get out there.

16 They are now regarded by industry and commerce as an exercise in independence and learning how to rely on oneself. Ten years ago, employers looked on gap years with suspicion but now they have a more positive attitude towards them. **17**

There are basically three ways of spending a gap year. **18** Most of these trips are short enough to be fitted into the summer vacation, but some can last up to six months. Unfortunately, many of the organisations only offer such projects for 18- and 19-year-olds although a few may encourage young adults of all ages to apply. **19** The cost of these trips can be fairly high, but people usually pay for some if not all of it through raising money from supporters.

The second way is the long holiday in which the student travels the world or a large part of it, perhaps working occasionally to add to spending money and pay for a new pair of trainers. **20** Overall, however, it seems risky to expect to find work once you are abroad and it is much better to arrange it beforehand. Student travel specialists such as Campus Travel arrange special student conditions with airlines that allow customers to change their ticket date and route. **21**

The final type of gap year involves choosing a part of the world in order to study or work in a particular area. **22** In this way people can develop skills and experience at an early age, which can lead to permanent employment after a few years when they return to their own country.

PART 4

You are going to read a newspaper article about activities for young people in the UK. For Questions **23-35**, choose from the activities described under the titles **(A-E)**. The titles may be chosen more than once. When more than one answer is required, these may be given in any order. There is an example at the beginning **(0)**.

Mark your answers **on the separate answer sheet**.

Which of the activity titles would you recommend for

someone who enjoys acting?	**0**	C
parents with young children under eight?	**23**	
	24	
someone who enjoys using their computer skills?	**25**	
a disabled person who wants to be sure of being included?	**26**	
people who enjoy feeling frightened?	**27**	
anyone who spends a lot of time watching television?	**28**	
someone who would like to see their children on a screen?	**29**	

Which of the activity titles suggests that

a person's character may benefit from the new experience?	**30**	
crowds of people can be a disadvantage?	**31**	
the future plays an important part in their design?	**32**	
	33	
the emphasis is on involving visitors as much as possible?	**34**	
	35	

There's No Need To Be Bored

Are your children hanging around and complaining they have nothing to do in the holidays? Here are some suggestions to help you keep them happy.

A Bad-Weather Sport

Children as young as four or five can learn to climb on indoor walls and need no special equipment to get started. In fact, even people who are blind or normally spend their lives in a wheelchair can enjoy some of the activities on offer. Young people gain a sense of responsibility and team skills through climbing, and at the same time may develop a real liking for a new pastime. Some of the indoor climbing centres have been established inside old buildings, and even experienced climbers find the artificial walls really exciting. The trick in learning to climb is to keep your weight on your feet and to keep looking down in order to see where to put your feet next. It's normal to feel frightened when you first start. But you have to focus your mind on what you're doing and not think about falling. For further information contact your local sports centre.

B Virtual Worlds

There is no point in trying to push youngsters into the fresh air if all they want to do is stay indoors and play with a computer. And, according to a recent report, there is no need to feel guilty when they do so – such games can help improve co-ordination skills and problem-solving abilities. The Trocadero in central London claims to be Europe's biggest indoor entertainment complex and is packed with high-tech excitement. The star attraction uses computer technology to fool you into thinking you are steering a small plane through an imaginary city in 2050. There is also a state-of-the-art electronic ride called Aqua Planet. Passengers are strapped into chairs, given special glasses and sent into a magical underwater world.

C Hands-on Museums

Not all museums are boring. There are now many museums which have interactive exhibits, that is exhibits which allow you to take part in various activities. For example, in one museum visitors can work on a production line in a factory or talk into a video-phone to find out what happens to the rubbish we throw out. If you want to be an astronaut, you can explore the solar system in a space workshop, and in another museum you can experience what an earthquake feels like – the ground really moves under your feet. There is even a theatre museum which holds workshops where teenagers can play the great romantic parts like Romeo or Juliet. Costumes are provided and the workshops are run by professional actors. This kind of activity is only suitable for fifteen to eighteen-year-olds, but there is one museum in the north of England which is specially suited to nine- to fourteen-year-olds. You can find out more about these and other hands-on museums by ringing 0071 22 54.

D The Great Outdoors

You don't have to wait for a fine day if you want to visit a theme park. Not far from London is a theme park full of exciting and adventurous rides. The main attraction is a new indoor ride which is suitable for anyone over the age of eight. This is the first ride of its kind in the world and involves a backward drop of fifteen metres in total darkness! You can book tickets for the theme park in advance, which is a good idea as it can get very busy. You should also try to arrive early in order to avoid the long queues for the rides which build up during the day. Another popular activity is a visit to a wild animal park. In most cases, the parks offer far more than just watching animals in the wild; very young children especially enjoy taking part in the feeding times for animals, which are usually advertised at the entrance to the park. Ring 0018 28571 for further details of parks in your area.

E TV Addicts

If you cannot drag your children away from the television, why not encourage them to explore the medium itself. There is a national museum of photography, film and television which allows visitors to develop their own photographic prints. In the same museum you can also visit a studio to see TV programmes being made. The star attraction, however, is the museum's five-storey Imax cinema, the only one of its kind in Britain, showing an amazing film of the US space shuttle. Another museum runs workshops which show how television and computers work and what cars will look like in a hundred years' time. Yet another museum allows children to design their own cartoon film or to watch a film of themselves being interviewed by a famous TV personality. You can find out more by contacting an information hotline on 00 11 848.

PAPER 2 Writing

1 hour 30 minutes

PART 1

You **must** answer this question.

1 A friend has written to you and sent you this advertisement for travel scholarships which he/she intends applying for. Below is an extract from your friend's letter.

Read all the information carefully, including the comments you have made. Write a letter to your friend pointing out the possible problems as well as making some suggestions.

Who are they?

This all seems very unlikely.

Apply now for one of our exciting travel scholarships!
Just fill in the application form below telling us where you would like to go, what you plan on doing and how much you think it will cost. Ring us today on 100 50 61 22 44 for more information.

I thought this would be brilliant - it's just what I'm looking for! Let me know what you think and I'll give them a ring as soon as I hear from you. I think I'll try and take at least a year off from my job and fit in as many countries as possible. If I can hitchhike, I'll be able to make the money go even further.

Are you serious?

After only 3 months in the job?!

Write a **letter** of between **120 and 180** words in an appropriate style.
Do not write any addresses.

9

PART 2

Write an answer to **one** of the Questions 2-5 in this part. Write your answer in **120-180** words in an appropriate style, putting the question number in the box.

2   An international magazine is asking young people of any nationality to send in articles which will be published in a special edition. The title of the article is:

What I hope to be doing in ten years' time

Write your **article**.

3   You have decided to enter a short-story competition. The rules of the competition are that your story must begin or end with the following words:

Chris stared out of the window waiting for the phone to ring.

Write your **story**.

4   You have been on a trip (for example to a museum, an exhibition or a festival). Your teacher has asked you to write a report for the rest of the class about your visit, giving your reasons as to whether the visit was worthwhile or not.

Write your **report**.

5   **Background reading texts**

Answer **one** of the following two questions based on your reading of **one** of the set books. Your answer should contain enough detail to make it clear to someone who may not have read the book. Write the letter **(a)** or **(b)** as well as the number **5** in the question box, and the **title** of the book next to the box.

Either   **(a)**   If you had to recommend the book which you have read, what would you say was most enjoyable and interesting about it and why?

Or   **(b)**   Describe the character(s) you found most interesting in the book which you have read and say whom you would most like to meet and why.

PAPER 3 Use of English

1 hour 15 minutes

For Questions **1-15**, read the text below and decide which answer **A**, **B**, **C** or **D** best fits each space. There is an example at the beginning **(0)**.

Mark your answers **on the separate answer sheet**.

Example:

| 0 | **A** doing | **B** making | **C** being | **D** having |

```
0   A   B   C   D
    ═   ═   ▬   ═
```

THE IDEAL INTERVIEW

When you are **(0)** ..... interviewed, 80 per cent of your mental effort **(1)** ..... into thinking about what to say and about 20 per cent into how to say it. The interviewer measures you the **(2)** ..... way round. According **(3)** ..... one expert, you **(4)** ..... to practise your role.

(5) ..... of confidence at an interview puts employers off, **(6)** ..... sit on a chair in front of a mirror before the interview and rearrange yourself **(7)** ..... you look confident. Make sure you sit up straight and do everything in a **(8)** ..... way. If you look forced, you will feel tense. Get **(9)** ..... to listen to your voice. If you are nervous, you are **(10)** ..... to talk in a dull tone. But if you talk faster **(11)** ..... you normally do, what comes out is likely to be nonsensical.

Nor do you want to be **(12)** ..... , which is why you need to practise. Vary the speed and the emphasis so you do not **(13)** ..... your interviewer. A good interviewer will **(14)** ..... open-ended questions, so try and **(15)** ..... answers which are clear and precise.

1	**A** falls	**B** puts	**C** breaks	**D** goes
2	**A** next	**B** other	**C** wrong	**D** best
3	**A** for	**B** by	**C** with	**D** to
4	**A** must	**B** need	**C** study	**D** got
5	**A** Lack	**B** Scarcity	**C** Failure	**D** Absence
6	**A** and	**B** when	**C** so	**D** but
7	**A** provided	**B** until	**C** while	**D** unless
8	**A** loose	**B** simple	**C** relaxed	**D** gentle
9	**A** someone	**B** them	**C** one	**D** him
10	**A** possibly	**B** really	**C** likely	**D** probably
11	**A** than	**B** as	**C** like	**D** then
12	**A** cautious	**B** unwilling	**C** doubtful	**D** hesitant
13	**A** hate	**B** bore	**C** disgust	**D** fail
14	**A** say	**B** give	**C** ask	**D** reply
15	**A** supply	**B** think	**C** support	**D** arrange

PART 2

For Questions **16-30**, read the text below and think of the word which best fits each space. Use only **one** word in each space. There is an example at the beginning **(0)**.

Write your answers **on the separate answer sheet**.

Example: | **0** | *the* |

NORTHERN LIGHTS

Aurora borealis – the northern lights – is one of **(0)** .... world's most magical firework displays. These displays **(16)** .... light are most intense around the North pole, so in **(17)** .... to experience them fully on a dark winter's night, you **(18)** .... ideally be in the Arctic Circle.

The lights are actually tiny glowing particles from the sun, travelling on a solar wind. **(19)** .... these particles come past the earth, they are trapped by **(20)** .... magnetic field and rapidly fall towards the pole. **(21)** .... the displays occur all year round, the number varies in **(22)** .... one year, depending **(23)** .... the sunspot cycle.

You need to be **(24)** .... from the glow of the city on a cloudless night to see the northern lights properly, and people **(25)** .... have witnessed them say they are unforgettable. At **(26)** .... brightest it's possible to read a book in the middle of the **(27)** .... as the whole area is lit up. Great sheets of light move across the sky in constantly-changing patterns **(28)** .... huge colourful curtains. **(29)** .... , you don't have to go to the ends of the earth to get a really good view of the lights. It's **(30)** .... to see the effect on dark nights from the far north of Scotland, especially from some of the northernmost islands.

PART 3

For Questions **31-40**, complete the second sentence so that it has a similar meaning to the first sentence, using the word given. **Do not change the word given.** You must use between two and five words, including the word given. Here is an example **(0)**.

Example:

0   The suitcase is not light enough for me to carry.

too

The suitcase .... for me to carry.

The gap can be filled by the words 'is too heavy' so you write:

0	is too heavy

Write **only** the missing words **on the separate answer sheet**.

---

31   Despite the heat Sam kept his jacket on.

of

In spite .... not take his jacket off.

32   Swimming in the river is forbidden.

allowed

You .... in the river.

33   Most of my neighbours travel to work in the city.

in

Most of the people .... travel to work in the city.

34   I'm really sorry I missed you when you were here.

regret

I .... you when you were here.

35 The apples were too sour to eat.

sweet

The apples were .... to eat.

36 Why did Gemma change her plans?

reason

What .... her change of plan?

37 I am not very interested in sport.

interest

Sport .... me.

38 My friends are bringing the music for the party.

being

The music for the party .... my friends.

39 If only I played a musical instrument.

could

I .... a musical instrument.

40 Unless you finish this work, you won't be able to go home.

if

You won't be able to go home .... this work.

PART 4

For Questions **41-55**, read the text below and look carefully at each line. Some of the lines are correct, and some have a word which should not be there.
If a line is correct, put a tick (✓) by the number **on the separate answer sheet**. If a line has a word which should not be there, write the word **on the separate answer sheet**. There are two examples at the beginning **(0)** and **(00)**.

Examples:

0	✓
00	it

AN INVITATION

Dear Claudia,

0	Thank you very much for your letter. I was really pleased to
00	hear it from you. The reason why I am writing back so soon
41	is because that I want to invite you to my party next week. As I told
42	you, I will be leaving for to study abroad very shortly and it
43	will also be my birthday in a couple of two weeks. So my family
44	has decided to hold one big party to celebrate both occasions!
45	We're inviting as many people as possible as we're having the
46	party in a local hotel. We've hired a band up for the evening and
47	we're planning a buffet supper. The party starts off at nine o'clock
48	and will go on until so late. If you can come, you are very welcome
49	to stay at our house overnight; in the fact, I think there will be quite
50	a lot of my friends staying the night! I'm sure you will remember
51	most of them from our schooldays, but my parents have to invited
52	family friends, too. I don't expect there will be another one opportunity
53	for everyone to get together. I shall be really disappointed if you're
54	unable to come there as you are my oldest and closest friend and it
55	won't be all the same without you.

PART 5

For Questions **56-65**, read the text below. Use the word given in capitals at the end of each line to form a word that fits in the space in the same line. There is an example at the beginning **(0)**.

Write your answers **on the separate answer sheet**.

Example: | **0** | *inventor* |

ERNO RUBIK

Erno Rubik is the well-known **(0)** *inventor* of the Rubik Cube, which sold over **INVENT**

100 million in its first ten years. He is one of the **(56)** ..... men in **WEALTHY**

Hungary and says that his most important tools are his **(57)** ..... **IMAGINE**

and his brain. He enjoys geometry and the problems of **(58)** ..... . **CONSTRUCT**

He says that he has many **(59)** ..... , who bring their dreams to him **VISIT**

and want him to turn them into **(60)** ..... , but it's his own dreams that **REAL**

really excite him.

Before he invented his famous Cube, he was a **(61)** ..... in interior **LECTURE**

design. Now he runs his own **(62)** ..... from an office in Budapest, but **ORGANISE**

is rarely seen in public. He is usually **(63)** ..... to appear on television or **WILL**

make guest **(64)** ..... anywhere, although one year he did agree to **APPEAR**

attend an **(65)** ..... of Hungarian design in London. **EXHIBIT**

PAPER 4   Listening

PART 1

You will hear people talking in eight different situations. For Questions **1-8**, choose the best answer, **A**, **B** or **C**.

---

1   You hear a woman talking to a supermarket manager.

     What is she complaining about?

     A   soft pears and lemons
     B   rotten oranges and apples | | **1** |
     C   brown lemons and grapes

2   You hear a man cancelling a hotel booking.

     What is the reason for the cancellation?

     A   His wife has to go into hospital.
     B   His wife has to go away suddenly. | | **2** |
     C   His wife has been in an accident.

3   You are visiting an art exhibition.

     What does your friend say about it?

     A   It's expensive.
     B   It's too modern. | | **3** |
     C   It's meaningless.

4   Listen to these two people talking.

     What are they discussing?

     A   a car
     B   a bike | | **4** |
     C   a fridge

5   Listen to a teacher talking to some students.

What is he telling them to do?

A   write down some information
B   look at a new film
C   copy out some information

	5

6   Listen to this radio advertisement.

What is being advertised?

A   package tours
B   home exchanges
C   luxury holidays

	6

7   You hear a man talking about why he decided to lose weight.

What is the reason he gives?

A   He felt overweight.
B   His clothes were very tight.
C   He couldn't stop eating.

	7

8   You overhear two people talking about a woman on their staff.

What is the problem?

A   She complains all the time.
B   She gets upset very easily.
C   She's always late for work.

	8

PART 2

You will hear a radio interview with a girl called Silvia, who has won a competition. For Questions **9-18**, complete the sentences.

---

9 Silvia won her first competition when [**9**] .

10 Her short story was published in [**10**] with others.

Background

11+ Her parents work as [**11**] and
12 [**12**] .

13 Her parents used to [**13**] at bedtime.

14 As a child she would [**14**] to other people.

15 Writing [**15**] is what she likes best.

Young Writer's Award

16 Her £1,000 prize will be used to buy [**16**] .

17 Her first novel will be read by [**17**] .

18 The best thing about the award is [**18**] she will receive.

PART 3

You will hear five different people apologising about something. For Questions **19-23**, choose from the list **A-F** the reason for each speaker's apology. Use the letters only once. There is one extra letter which you do not need to use.

A   disturbing someone

Speaker 1   [| **19**]

B   cancelling a theatre booking

Speaker 2   [| **20**]

C   leaving something behind

Speaker 3   [| **21**]

D   forgetting to write something down

Speaker 4   [| **22**]

E   arriving very late

Speaker 5   [| **23**]

F   dropping something

PART 4

You will hear a conversation which takes place in a café between three friends – Anna, Peter and Miriam – who used to be at school together.

Answer questions **24-30** by writing   **A** (for Anna)

P (for Peter) or

M (for Miriam) in the boxes provided.

24   Who has a reputation for not being on time? | 24 |

25   Who complains about work? | 25 |

26   Who made a disappointing choice? | 26 |

27   Who is sympathetic? | 27 |

28   Who feels the most positive? | 28 |

29   Who regrets rushing into a decision? | 29 |

30   Who is uncertain about the future? | 30 |

PAPER 5   The Speaking Test

PART 1   (3 MINUTES)

The teacher (interlocutor) invites each candidate to speak in turn and give personal information about themselves.

Candidates can expect a variety of questions, some of which will require short answers, and some requiring longer answers about their present circumstances, past experiences and future plans, such as:

Where do you come from?

Have you always lived there / here?

Can you tell us what it's like?

What do you usually do in your spare time?

What are you hoping to do when you leave school / college?

What are your plans for the future?

Candidates talk to each other and the interlocutor.

PART 2   (4 MINUTES)

Teacher   Now I'm going to give each of you two different photographs. I'd like you both to show each other your pictures and then talk about them.

You each have a minute for this part, so don't worry if I interrupt you.

X, here are your two pictures. Let **Y** have a look at them. They are both photographs of street entertainers.

(Show photos 1 and 2 to X.)

Y, I'll show you your photos in a minute.

Now **X**, I'd like you to compare and contrast your photos and talk about which kind of entertainment you would prefer.

Remember, you have about a minute for this.

(Allow about a minute for X to talk without interruption.)

Thank you. **Y**, which of these entertainers would you prefer to watch?

(Allow Y about 20 seconds.)

Thank you. Now **Y**, here are your photographs. Let **X** have a look at them. They both show people on their own.

(Show photos 3 and 4 to Y.)

Now **Y**, I'd like you to compare and contrast your photos and say what you think about the elderly people in the pictures.

Remember, you have about a minute for this.

(Allow about a minute for Y to talk without interruption.)

Thank you. Now **X**, what would you suggest an old person could do if he / she felt lonely?

(Allow X about 20 seconds.)

Thank you.

PART 3 (3 MINUTES)

Teacher   I want you to imagine that you have to design a poster for tourists who visit your town, warning them to look after their possessions.

*(Show picture 5 to **X** and **Y**.)*

I want you to talk to each other and decide which **3** pictures you think it would be most useful to include and why.

You have about three minutes to talk to each other, so don't worry if I stop you.

*(Allow **X** and **Y** about 3 minutes.)*

Thank you.

PART 4 (4 MINUTES)

Teacher   Do you think this kind of advice is important? Why? / Why not?

Do you think if tourists see this kind of information, it will make them feel unnecessarily nervous?

Is there anything else which you think should be included on this poster?

Do you think newspaper and television reports of crime should be given less attention? Why? / Why not?

Do you think that living in the country is safer than living in a city? Why? / Why not?

Thank you. That is the end.

Practice Test 2

PAPER 1   Reading

PART 1

You are going to read a newspaper article about education. Choose the most suitable heading from the list **A-I** for each part **(1-7)** of the article. There is one extra heading which you do not need to use. There is an example at the beginning **(0)**.

Mark your answers **on the separate answer sheet**.

A	Learning about new technology
B	Fresh approach to teaching required
C	The results of technological change
D	Where people's money goes
E	Older workers' skills out of date
F	A new kind of student
G	People slow to recognise change
H	Two possible ways forward
I	Making up for what was missed in the past

Return to School

The ageing population has time, money and a will to learn, reports Robert Nurden.

0	F

A quiet revolution is altering the face of adult education across Europe. Various social factors have combined to create a class of learners with time on their hands, money to spend and a thirst for knowledge. They have become the new generation of the eternal student: they are the over-50s, and by the year 2026, experts predict, half the population of Europe will be over 55.

1	

Technology now does much of the work in certain industries which was previously done by clerical staff. Consequently, tens of thousands of people in their 50s have been made redundant and found themselves without a job or forced to take early retirement.

2	

The return to education for these people falls into one of two groups. They either retrain in a new area in order to increase their chances of getting another job or, having given up all hope of working again, they return to education to pursue a personal interest.

3	

For many, however, the return to education is not out of choice: they would prefer to be working. But computer technology has left this older generation behind, and their experience is of less value than the youthful quick-fix thinking of young people brought up with this new technology.

4	

It is interesting that one of the most popular courses taken by Third Age students is information technology. They see their PC as an effective way of communicating, but first they must know how to use it.

5	

Another important reason for the Third Age education explosion is that it provides many people with a second chance. Women in particular are seizing the opportunity, and those who never went on to higher education make up a proportion of 'late' students.

6	

People over 55 years of age control about two thirds of western Europe's savings. They have large amounts of money which is spent largely on leisure activities. The taking of holidays – increasingly study holidays – and the buying of second homes are popular ways of spending money. For many people the second home is in another country, in which case they are keen to learn the local language. If they decide to make a permanent move to another country, then the success of such a move will largely depend on their ability to speak the language really well.

7	

This changing pattern of behaviour is affecting teachers and especially writers of language course materials. The current materials are often unsuitable for older students. They resist the fashionable content of many of today's textbooks, preferring a more grammatical approach.

PART 2

You are going to read an article about Yehudi Menuhin, the musician, who was born in New York of Russian parents. For Questions **8-15**, choose the answer (**A**, **B**, **C** or **D**) which you think fits best according to the text.

Mark your answers **on the separate answer sheet**.

Being a touring musician is bit like being a sailor. It's constant motion, a continuous routine of settling into new hotels and meeting new people. So my ideal holiday is enjoying being alone with my wife.

My earliest memory of a holiday was when I was five. We had just bought our first car, and drove joyously from San Francisco, exploring the most beautiful parts of California. It was a wonderful experience. I vividly remember the beautiful Yosemite valley, a place of waterfalls and haunting mountains, a wilderness before we polluted it with cars and noisy stereo systems.

line 12

As a child I collected photographs of those huge railway engines that pulled hundreds of goods wagons across America. These trains were like monsters, with groups of four wheels on each side. For Americans trains are hugely romantic. My first train journey across America was when I was eight years old. During the day I sat at the window watching the scenery fly past. At night I always had the top bunk bed in the sleeping compartment. I would scramble up to read in bed, feeling cosy and contented as the train rhythmically travelled over the rails through the night.

Since then I've worked and studied for many hours on trains, enjoying the view and the sense of timelessness. I loved the smell of steel upon steel mixed up with the smell of the countryside. I loved the sound of the engine's horn, which used to remind me of the ferries which crept along in between the ships in San Francisco Bay on foggy nights.

I have been lucky travelling all over the world and managing, just occasionally, to take a few days actually to see something more than just the airport, hotel and concert hall. When my wife and I were in Peru, we took three days off and flew in a small plane to the mountains where we spent a wonderful time walking and exploring in the jungle.

Forty years ago we bought a small house on a Greek island and went there whenever we could. Initially there were just a few carts, and everything was transported on the back of a donkey or a man. We had a tiny cottage with a lovely garden of fruit trees where we used to pick grapes and oranges. We spent a lot of time on the beach – as I love swimming – and in the village getting to know people. After ten or fifteen years we were firmly involved in the community, able to share a totally different world, different language, different music.

8 Why does Yehudi Menuhin compare his life to that of a sailor?
A He has a definite routine.
B He's always meeting people.
C He can't be with his wife.
D He's always on the move.

9 What does 'it' in line 12 refer to?
A his touring holiday in California
B his wonderful experience
C the Californian wilderness
D the beautiful Yosemite valley

10 The young Menuhin thought American trains were
A enormous.
B noisy.
C smelly.
D terrifying.

11 What does Menuhln say about travelling by train at night?
A He enjoyed listening to the sounds.
B He found night-time scenery exciting.
C He felt warm, safe and comfortable.
D He specially enjoyed the sense of rhythm.

12 Which word in the fourth paragraph suggests a link with one of the ideas expressed in the first paragraph?
A nights
B ships
C trains
D countryside

13 What does Menuhin seem to appreciate most about his life?
A taking time off whenever he wants
B visiting a variety of different places
C exploring wild and distant places
D being able to travel with his family

14 What does Menuhin suggest about village life on a Greek island?
A It is easy to become part of the community.
B Its people are very kind and welcoming.
C It takes time to become part of the community.
D It is lonely and cut off from the rest of the world.

15 What is the writer's purpose in this text?
A to describe what it's like to be a musician
B to share his early childhood experiences
C to look back over his various foreign holidays
D to encourage people to share his love of travel

PART 3

You are going to read a newspaper article about a little-known sport called korfball. Seven sentences have been removed from the article. Choose from the sentences **A-H** the one which fits each gap **(16-21)**. There is one extra sentence which you do not need to use. There is an example at the beginning **(0)**.

Mark your answers **on the separate answer sheet**.

A   Play, therefore, can continue when a shot is missed.

B   The game was adapted by a Dutch teacher in a mixed school in Amsterdam, from a game he saw being played in southern Sweden in 1902.

C   In Taiwan the game even receives government funding.

D   If you touch the lines around your division, you are breaking the rules.

E   The day may then come when people stop asking, 'You play what?'

F   Players are not allowed to run with the ball so the use of space and movement away from your opponent are important.

G   By definition korfball must be played by mixed teams and is a handball game of speed and immense variety.

H   Moreover in 1987 a national league was formed in the UK which now attracts around 4,000 players in more than thirty centres.

It's not a basket or a net, it's a korf

In 1996 korfball celebrated its fiftieth birthday in London with a special match – and very few people noticed.

| 0 | B | In 1920 the game was demonstrated at the Olympic Games in Belgium and in 1946 Dutch players demonstrated the game for the first time in the UK. Although it became established in south-east London, its development was very limited. However, in the last fifteen years the development of korfball has been very impressive worldwide. | 16 | Interestingly, most of these centres are in university towns.

| 17 | In order to describe it to the vast majority who have never heard of the game, it is best defined as a mixture of basketball and netball. The pitch is rectangular and measures 40 metres by 20 metres indoors or 60 metres by 30 metres on grass, and is divided into two like a football pitch. | 18 |

There are eight players in a team; two men and two women play in defence and the same numbers in attack, but after every two goals – scored by either team – the players change divisions, and roles: attackers become defenders and defenders become attackers. | 19 | Since it is very much a team game, to succeed at the top level individuals require balance, speed and the ability to think ahead and move into space.

The most recent world championship was held in India in 1995, and internationally korfball is established in more than fifty countries. It has recently been given full membership of the Olympic movement, and in magazines there have been articles about the game in various countries from Australia to Russia, South Africa to the USA. | 20 |

It may have taken a very long time to lay the foundations of the game, but with Olympic recognition perhaps in the not-too-distant future, korfball seems set to expand. | 21 |

PART 4

You are going to read some information about theme parks. For Questions **22-35**, choose from the theme parks **(A-E)**. The theme parks may be chosen more than once. When more than one answer is required, these may be given in any order. There is an example at the beginning **(0)**.

Mark your answers **on the separate answer sheet**.

Which of the theme parks

charges the same price for adults and children?	**0**	E
is particularly suitable for young children?	**22**	
provides an interesting way in?	**23**	
is just as attractive without any rides?	**24**	
uses films for its themes?	**25**	
offers frightening rides through water?	**26**	
	27	
seems most appropriate for adults?	**28**	
is based on tales and stories?	**29**	
is by the sea?	**30**	
	31	
charges separately for each ride?	**32**	
apparently appeals to everyone?	**33**	
has the sharpest water drop?	**34**	
offers the greatest variety or different locations for its rides?	**35**	

The Pick of the World's Theme Parks

A   Universal Studios – Hollywood

Seen the movie? Now try the ride. Jurassic Park opened in June 1996 at a cost of $110 million. Described as 'the most technically advanced interactive themed ride in entertainment history', Jurassic Park has five-storey-tall monsters, miracles of modern bio-engineering, which come to within inches of your eyebrows. You cruise in a boat through a tropical forest, ending up diving into a pitch-dark lagoon; it is the fastest, steepest water drop in amusement park history. A lifetime of primeval terror packed into five and a half minutes.   Among the other 'star' attractions is WaterWorld, based on the movie and the nearest you can get to giant fireballs, exploding seaplanes and other disasters. There are also other favourites such as King Kong, Jaws, ET and Back to the Future, a journey from the Ice Age to 2015. More for grown-ups, perhaps, than children.

Entry details: $34 for adults, $26 for children.

B   Sentosa – Singapore

For families stopping over in Singapore on the way to Australia, Sentosa is the perfect place. Two of the newest attractions are VolcanoLand, offering a journey to the centre of the Earth with half-hourly volcanic explosions, bursts of hot air and trembling floors, and WonderGolf, full of waterfalls and other obstacles. Sentosa also has the largest aquarium in south-east Asia, a Fantasy Island water park with 32 rides, and several Chinese heritage performances from traditional wedding ceremonies to firewalking. There is also a butterfly park and insect kingdom. Part of the pleasure of Sentosa is getting there, on foot or by bus across a raised causeway, by the four-minute ferry ride or, most excitingly, by cable car.

Entry details: Everything is individually priced from $2–$14 for adults, roughly half for children, in addition to the $6 ($4) entry fee.

C   Legoland – Denmark

Legoland falls into two camps. One is Miniland, where places such as Amsterdam, Copenhagen harbour and an English village stand as high a youngster's kneecap, each packed with detail and moving parts. There are also larger Lego figures all around the park, including Mount Rushmore, the Taj Mahal and Big Chief Sitting Bull, made of 1.5 million Lego bits. The other aspect of Legoland, the rides, are not spectacular but just right for little children. There is a sky railway, a mini driving school, helicopter rides and a boat ride through dark tunnels.

Entry details: Adults 100 Danish krone, children 90 krone.

D   Port Aventura – Spain

This theme park on the coast is situated near Salou on the Costa Dorada. Visitors can travel through five exotic lands: rural Spain, Polynesia, China, Mexico and the Wild West. The journeys are made by steam train, canoe, Chinese junk or on foot. People who feel brave can try the Dragon Khan rollercoaster which turns you upside down eight times. But the biggest demand is for a ride called the Tu Tu Ki Splash, a watery drop in an open-topped bus straight into a Polynesian lake.

Entry details: Adults 3,900 pesetas, children 3,000 pesetas.

E   Efteling – Holland

Once upon a time, 44 years ago, a Dutch artist started to build a magical land, bringing his own drawings to life. His Fairy Tale Forest is still at the heart of this timeless park of traditional tales and legends set in large woodlands. Efteling is visited by 2.5 million people each year and is an everything-to-all-ages sort of place. It is best known for its so-called dark rides, like Fata Morgana, a boat ride to a forbidden city through swamps and jungles. Even if you took the theme park out of Efteling, you would still be left with a lovely park where visitors are encouraged to bring a picnic.

Entry details: Adults and children both pay 32.50 guilders (under-4s free).

PAPER 2   Writing

PART 1

You **must** answer this question.

1   You are going to spend six months working in England. You are trying to find somewhere to live and you have received the following information from the Eagle Accommodation Agency, and a letter your English friend has sent you reminding you about various things.

Read the advertisement and the letter carefully. Then write a letter to the agency asking for further details which you need before you agree to rent accommodation through them, including any other things which you need to know in addition.

Eagle Accommodation Agency

— let us find you somewhere to live!

- **We specialise in finding first-class flats and bedsits for overseas visitors.**

- Share accommodation and cut the cost
- Excellent residential areas
- Close to public transport
- Weekly or monthly basis – reduction for stays of 3 months or more
- Reasonable prices
- Initial registration charge + deposit

> so do make sure you check the details, especially the total cost – some agencies are far more expensive than others. As you'll be coming during the winter months, you should also check on heating etc. and if you're going to share, I expect there'll be plenty of things you'll want to ask. Let me know if there's anything else I can do to help

Write a **letter** of between **120 and 180** words in an appropriate style.
Do not write any addresses.

PART 2

Write an answer to **one** of the Questions **2-5** in this part. Write your answer in **120-180** words in an appropriate style, putting the question number in the box.

2   Your school is going to offer courses in as many different languages as possible next year. As part of its advertising brochure it will include examples of students' work on the following topic:

The importance of learning foreign languages in today's world

Write your **composition**.

3   Some English friends are coming to stay with you for a weekend. They want to know about some of the tourist attractions which are available in your area, and have asked for two or three suggestions of things which you think they would especially enjoy doing.

Write your **letter**. Do not write any addresses.

4   An international magazine is running a competition which asks readers to write about an experience which has had an important influence on their life.

Write your **article**.

5   **Background reading texts**

Answer **one** of the following two questions based on your reading of **one** of the set books. Your answer should contain enough detail to make it clear to someone who may not have read the book. Write the letter **(a)** or **(b)** as well as the number **5** in the question box, and the **title** of the book next to the box.

Either   **(a)**   Describe one of the events in the book which you have read and say why you have chosen it and what you found memorable about it.

Or   **(b)**   Do you think the book which you have read would be suitable for a radio or television play? Explain why or why not.

PAPER 3   Use of English

PART 1

For Questions **1-15**, read the text below and decide which answer **A**, **B**, **C** or **D** best fits each space. There is an example at the beginning **(0)**.

Mark your answers **on the separate answer sheet**.

Example:

| 0 | **A** such | **B** as | **C** well | **D** like |

| 0 | A   B   C   D |

HIGH DAYS AND HOLIDAYS

In the UK holidays began **(0)** ..... religious festival days or 'holy days'. The idea of a holiday as a 'no-work' day seems to have first **(1)** ..... around five hundred years ago. In 1871 the Bank Holidays Act established **(2)** ..... days when, by law, banks closed. Bank Holidays soon **(3)** ..... public holidays, but by **(4)** ..... , not law.

Until this century working people **(5)** ..... took holidays. In fact, for some, paid holidays remained a **(6)** ..... until the second half of the twentieth century. Instead, people enjoyed outings for the day to **(7)** ..... places.

The **(8)** ..... of the railways made it possible for working people and their families to go further afield on their day trips, **(9)** ..... wealthy people had, for many years, taken holidays. As **(10)** ..... as outings became possible for more people, **(11)** ..... of them travelled to the seaside. Seaside towns started to boom. Piers were built out over the sea, funfairs opened and boat trips were **(12)** ..... by local fishermen. Many of the towns that **(13)** ..... from all these day trippers were near to large cities or were at the **(14)** ..... of railway lines. Towns such as Blackpool in the north of England and Brighton in the south have **(15)** ..... popular destinations.

1   **A** appeared   **B** grown   **C** come   **D** arrived

2   **A** absolute   **B** certain   **C** odd   **D** possible

3   **A** developed   **B** happened   **C** became   **D** turned

4   **A** habit   **B** tradition   **C** practice   **D** desire

5   **A** rarely   **B** quite   **C** gradually   **D** ever

6   **A** prize   **B** comfort   **C** reward   **D** luxury

7   **A** close   **B** away   **C** nearby   **D** next

8   **A** rise   **B** growth   **C** increase   **D** size

9   **A** because   **B** so   **C** although   **D** despite

10 **A** far   **B** soon   **C** early   **D** good

11 **A** piles   **B** rows   **C** crowds   **D** blocks

12 **A** done   **B** offered   **C** performed   **D** raised

13 **A** benefited   **B** advantaged   **C** helped   **D** achieved

14 **A** point   **B** stop   **C** completion   **D** end

15 **A** rested   **B** remained   **C** continued   **D** lasted

PART 2

For Questions **16-30**, read the text below and think of the word which best fits each space. Use only one word in each space. There is an example at the beginning **(0)**.

Write your answers **on the separate answer sheet**.

Example: | 0 | *over* |

SUPERMARKETS

Of all the revolutionary changes in our lives **(0)** .... the past fifty years, the introduction of supermarket shopping is surely **(16)** .... most significant. Although it is less **(17)** .... fifty years since the first self-service store opened **(18)** .... doors in south London, **(19)** .... most of us nowadays the supermarket plays an important **(20)** .... in our daily lives. **(21)** .... fact, some people's support of a particular supermarket can be **(22)** .... strong as their support of their favourite football club.

Layout and image are of vital importance for any supermarket. Fruit, vegetables, flowers and house-plants are usually displayed immediately inside the **(23)** .... to the store, **(24)** .... the fact that the majority of goods sold by a supermarket are frozen, tinned or preserved. This suggests an image **(25)** .... freshness, healthy eating and even 'greenness'. We are led **(26)** .... tempting displays to the basics – tea, bread, sugar, eggs – which are frequently placed well apart and **(27)** .... the back of the store. This trick encourages us **(28)** .... buy overpriced products in attractive packets and boxes.

We all know this, **(29)** .... in a strange way we love supermarkets. In the absence of anything else **(30)** .... unites us, it is a shared experience.

PART 3

For Questions **31-40**, complete the second sentence so that it has a similar meaning to the first sentence, using the word given. **Do not change the word given.** You must use between two and five words, including the word given. Here is an example **(0)**.

Example:

0 The suitcase is not light enough for me to carry.

too

The suitcase .... for me to carry.

The gap can be filled by the words 'is too heavy' so you write:

0	is too heavy

Write **only** the missing words **on the separate answer sheet**.

---

31 Strong winds prevented the ship from sailing.

was

The ship .... strong winds.

32 Lia had not seen such beautiful flowers before.

most

They were .... had seen.

33 I have finally decided to emigrate.

mind

I have finally .... emigrate.

34 Can you tell me the time?

what

Do .... is?

35 Andreas doesn't like people to interupt him when he's speaking.

objects

Andreas .... him when he's speaking.

36 I packed warm clothes for the trip as I thought the weather might get cold.

case

I packed warm clothes for the trip .... cold.

37 Monique said it was my fault that she missed her train.

blamed

Monique .... train.

38 Ben found it difficult to use a computer.

had

Ben .... a computer.

39 If you are not satisfied, complain to the manager.

make

Unless you .... to the manager.

40 I was horrified to find my home had been burgled.

horror

To .... that my home had been burgled.

PART 4

For Questions **41-55**, read the text below and look carefully at each line. Some of the lines are correct, and some have a word which should not be there.
If a line is correct, put a tick (✓) by the number **on the separate answer sheet**. If a line has a word which should not be there, write the word **on the separate answer sheet**. There are two examples at the beginning **(0 and 00)**.

Examples:

0	✓
00	since

ANCIENT CHEWING GUM

0   Chewing gum is often thought of as a nineteenth-century American invention.

00   However, recent research shows that chewing has been going on for since

41   at least ten thousand years. Apparently, young people thousands of the

42   years ago chewed a smoky-flavoured chewing gum made from the bark

43   of a tree. The substance was like to a black glue and when children had

44   had enough, they did spat it out. Samples of the ancient gum have been

45   found in Sweden, Germany, Denmark and Norway. Some samples have

46   teeth marks, which shows that the majority of users were aged in between

47   six and fifteeen. It is also possible so that the gum had pain-killing powers

48   and was used to treat toothache.The fact that children often chewed the

49   gum then at the age when they would have been losing their first teeth

50   suggests that they may have been trying to remove away loose teeth.

51   There is one fact, however, which is puzzling scientists. How was the

52   bark of the tree turned out into this black glue? The bark would need to

53   be heated to at least 80°C in an airtight pot, and this process was not

54   used until much later. Attempts by scientists to reproduce the process

55   by placing the bark on too hot stones in a hole have failed.

PART 5

For Questions **56-65**, read the text below. Use the word given in capitals at the end of each line to form a word that fits in the space in the same line. There is an example at the beginning **(0)**.

Write your answers **on the separate answer sheet**.

Example: | **0** | *dramatic* |

JEAN PIERRE BASSIN

Jean Pierre Bassin is an 'action cameraman' who films **(0)** *dramatic* events   **DRAMA**

like snowboarding or paragliding. His **(56)** ..... is using a video camera   **SPECIAL**

while skiing at high speed. His most recent **(57)** ..... was filming athletes   **ASSIGN**

at high altitudes. 'Everything is **(58)** ..... at this height,' he says. 'You   **EXHAUST**

take your **(59)** ..... out of the case and you're out of breath already.   **EQUIP**

I'm **(60)** ..... fit and I managed to take some shots running alonside the   **REASON**

athletes, but it was very hard. I had **(61)** ..... every morning and evening   **HEAD**

as well as **(62)** ..... nights.'   **SLEEP**

Jean Pierre is relaxed about how **(63)** ..... he has become and has few   **SUCCESS**

plans for the future. 'I'm not really interested in **(64)** ..... and my lifestyle is of   **BUSY**

greater **(65)** ..... than what's in my bank account.'   **IMPORTANT**

PAPER 4 Listening

PART 1

You will hear people talking in eight different situations. For Questions **1-8**, choose the best answer, **A**, **B** or **C**.

---

1   You hear a woman talking on the phone.

Who is she talking to?

A   a store assistant

B   a store manager

C   a store director

	1

2   You hear a woman talking to a friend.

Where has she been?

A   a music class

B   an exercise class

C   a swimming class

	2

3   You overhear a man talking to his friend.

What are they planning to do?

A   buy a house in the country

B   go away for a holiday

C   change where they work

	3

4   Listen to this radio announcement.

What is the next programme about?

A   food

B   chemistry

C   cookery

	4

5   Listen to a policeman talking to some people.

What is about to happen?

   A   There's going to be a concert.

   B   There's going to be a parade.

   C   There's going to be a match.

	5

6   You hear a man telling someone about a recent experience in a theatre.

What had happened?

   A   His seat broke during the performance.

   B   He was given a free seat for the show.

   C   His seat was broken when he arrived.

	6

7   Listen to this woman explaining why she is late.

What is the reason she gives?

   A   Two trains were withdrawn.

   B   The drivers were on strike.

   C   She missed her first train.

	7

8   You hear two people talking about their work.

What kind of work do they do?

   A   They make bread.

   B   They work in a hospital.

   C   They clean offices.

	8

PART 2

You will hear a travel company representative called Samantha talking to some hotel guests at the start of their holiday. For Questions **9-18**, complete the notes.

9 Samantha shares an office with:

| | 9 |

10 In emergencies, contact Samantha through:

| | 10 |

11 In case of illness, ask for:

| | 11 |

12 Essential to book day excursions:

| | 12 |

13 Excursion to Mount Sispi, take:

| | 13 |

14 Reductions for hotel guests at:

| | 14 |

15 Many shops don't close:

| | 15 |

16 Extra charge made for using:

| | 16 |

17 Disobeying traffic rules means instant:

| | 17 |

18 Official taxis are yellow and have:

| | 18 |

PART 3

You will hear five different people talking about being the eldest child in a family. For Questions **19-23**, choose from the list **A-F** the best thing each speaker remembers about being the eldest. Use the letters only once. There is one extra letter which you do not need to use.

A   feeling certain of oneself

Speaker 1		19

B   not arguing with parents

Speaker 2		20

C   having parental attention

Speaker 3		21

D   learning to be supportive

Speaker 4		22

E   being bought new clothes

Speaker 5		23

F   enjoying special advantages

PART 4

You will hear part of an interview with two young people, Mariko and Ronan. For Questions **24-30**, choose the best answer, **A**, **B** or **C**.

---

24   *The Dreamers* is a radio programme which

  A   helps young people achieve dreams.

  B   discusses young people's hopes.

  C   interviews successful young people.

| | 24 |

25   The woman in the supermarket

  A   offered Mariko a good modelling job.

  B   suggested Mariko moved to London.

  C   told Mariko she had modelling ability.

| | 25 |

26   Mariko found the big London agency

  A   depressing.

  B   unhelpful

  C   frightening.

| | 26 |

27   What is Mariko's attitude towards her future?

  A   She feels uncertain.

  B   She feels positive.

  C   She feels overworked.

| | 27 |

28   What happened first when Ronan left school?

  A   He was unemployed.

  B   He went to college.

  C   He worked in a shop.

| | 28 |

29   Ronan was offered a job because he

  A   looked so desperate.

  B   took an opportunity.

  C   seemed very friendly.

| | 29 |

30   Why was Ronan offered the business?

  A   The owner's son was not interested.

  B   The shopkeepers preferred his work.

  C   The owner was fed up with running it.

| | 30 |

PAPER 5   The Speaking Test

PART 1   (3 MINUTES)

The teacher (interlocutor) invites each candidate to speak in turn and give personal information about themselves.

Candidates can expect a variety of questions, some of which will require short answers, and some requiring longer answers about their present circumstances, past experiences and their future plans, such as:

Whereabouts in (name of town or city if student lives locally) do you live?

What are the good and bad points about living here / there?

What are your favourite subjects at school? / What does your job involve?

How do you usually spend your holidays?

What are you hoping to do when you leave school / college?

What are your plans for the future?

Candidates talk to each other and the interlocutor.

PART 2   (4 MINUTES)

Teacher   Now I'm going to give each of you two different photographs. I'd like you both to show each other your pictures and then talk about them.

You each have a minute for this part, so don't worry if I interrupt you.

X, here are your two pictures. Let **Y** have a look at them. They are both photographs of young people.

*(Show photos 1 and 2 to **X**.)*

Y, I'll show you your photos in a minute.

Now **X**, I'd like you to compare and contrast your photos and talk about the kind of lives you think these young people lead.

Remember, you have about a minute for this.

*(Allow about a minute for **X** to talk without interruption.)*

Thank you. **Y**, which of these lifestyles appeals to you?

*(Allow **Y** about 20 seconds.)*

Thank you. Now **Y**, here are your photographs. Let **X** have a look at them. They both show people doing things.

*(Show photos 3 and 4 to **Y**.)*

Now **Y**, I'd like you to compare and contrast your photos and say what you think the different people are doing in the pictures.

Remember, you have about a minute for this.

*(Allow about a minute for **Y** to talk without interruption.)*

Thank you. Now **X**, what sort of things do you like to do in your spare time?

*(Allow **X** about 20 seconds.)*

Thank you.

PART 3 (3 MINUTES)

Teacher I want you to imagine that you have won a lot of money. Here are some pictures of things that you can do with the money.

(Show picture 5 to X and Y.)

I want you to talk to each other and decide which **3** things you would spend the money on and why.

You have about three minutes to talk to each other, so don't worry if I stop you.

(Allow X and Y about 3 minutes.)

Thank you.

PART 4 (4 MINUTES)

Teacher Do you think that having a lot of money could be a disadvantage? Why? / Why not?

Do you think that there is any connection between money and happiness? In what way(s)?

Is there anything else which you would want to spend the money on which is not included in the pictures?

Do you think money has too much importance in our society? Why? / Why not?

Would you like to see a society where everyone earned more or less the same? Why? / Why not?

Thank you. That is the end.

Practice Test 3

PART 1

You are going to read a newspaper article about the importance of language for airlines. Choose the most suitable summary sentence from the list **A-I** for each part **(1-7)** of the article. There is one extra summary sentence which you do not need to use. There is an example at the beginning **(0)**.

Mark your answers **on the separate answer sheet**.

A	Pilots only need a limited technical vocabulary.
B	Misunderstandings arise from even basic words.
C	The skies are crowded and the staff poorly trained.
D	Communication may use more technology in future.
E	The importance of English in the air should not be neglected.
F	An unexpected crisis can cause language problems.
G	An artificial language may be developed.
H	There is a strong language link between safety and flying.
I	High training standards exist for some employees.

The Language of Flying

How can we be sure that all pilots have the right language skills?

0	H

English is universally accepted by airlines these days as the standard language of aviation. But people's understanding and command of the language vary, and although serious mistakes are rare, accidents can be caused by linguistic mix-ups.

1	

In the past ten years, two new factors have made communication in the skies more problematical. One is the increase in the number of international routes from countries where the air crews have not had adequate language training. The other is the commercial pressure on airlines: every second an aircraft spends on the ground costs money and so the skies are becoming even busier.

2	

In some countries, airlines insist that applicants should have excellent English at the interview stage. They have to sit an exam which tests speaking, listening and written skills. Staff then have to attend a strict teaching programme to learn the specialist language of flying.

3	

In other countries, although the procedures are similar, there may not be enough native speakers of English to do the training. Pilots are only required to know about 300–350 specialist flying words in English, and every switch in the cockpit, or the pilot's cabin, is labelled in English.

4	

However, an emergency puts language under pressure and people's language control may slip. If pilots only know the technical language for flying an aeroplane, they will not be able to deal with an emergency.

5	

The following example shows how ordinary language can be even more important than technical language. If a pilot says, 'We are now at take-off,' an air traffic controller may understand this to mean that the plane is waiting at the take-off point for further instructions. If, however, the pilot means that he is actually in the process of taking off, then the risk of an accident increases as a result of a relatively simple language mistake.

6	

One suggestion as to how this problem can be overcome would be to develop a machine which would act like an 'intelligent voice' and sort out any language confusion. This machine would be programmed to speak the standard aviation phrases used by pilots all over the world. A pilot would only have to press the right switch to send a message instead of speaking, and the machine would hear the message and send the appropriate reply to the pilot.

7	

The International Civil Aviation Organisation (ICAO) is even considering inventing a new language. It would be based on English but include features from various other languages.

PART 2

You are going to read an extract from an article about sending an orchestra abroad. For Questions **8-15**, choose the answer (**A**, **B**, **C** or **D**) which you think fits best according to the text.

Mark your answers **on the separate answer sheet**.

'Footballers and musicians are in the same business. They both do stressful jobs in front of critical audiences. The only difference is that football crowds are noisier.' So says Rod Franks. And he should know. Franks started his working life with Leeds United Football Club, neatly changed direction, started playing the trumpet instead of football, and is now principal trumpeter with the LSO (London Symphony Orchestra). Franks might have made a further observation about the similarities between orchestras and football clubs: it is playing away that presents the real challenges.

London's oldest orchestra has been playing away since it was formed almost a century ago. Nowadays, the orchestra's trips abroad are kept to tours of a maximum of two and a half weeks. But since touring is clearly expensive and presents major organisational and technical problems, why bother to tour at all? Clive Gillinson, the managing director, says: 'A great international orchestra needs to work with the greatest conductors and soloists. No recording company will record a conductor or soloist if he or she is only known in one territory – they need an international reputation. So for the recording side to work, you have to visit the key markets; you need to tour.'

By touring with projects or festivals, Gillinson is able to create an event, not just provide a series of concerts. It is more expensive to do, but when you leave town you are not so easily forgotten. line 30

For Sue Mallet, the orchestra's administrator, the difficulties of her job lie in getting a symphony orchestra and its instruments on stage, on time and in one piece. However well she plans each tour, and she does her planning with scientific accuracy, line 36 events sometimes take an upper hand. On one occasion a concert had been advertised for the wrong night, and on another the lorry carrying the instruments from the airport to the concert hall broke down and got stuck in snow.

It is a tiring and stressful business flying around the world, and yet on balance it is one of the rewards of the job. Certain moments are unforgettable. At the end of a concert in Moscow line 45 an enthusiastic audience had brought the orchestra to its feet. As one of the musicians was about to sit down, an elderly lady in the front row pressed a piece of paper into his hand. It said, in words of simple English, what lovely music the orchestra had made.

8 What do footballers and musicians have in common?

   A Their work abroad earns a lot of praise.

   B They receive too much unfair criticism.

   C They enjoy extremely noisy audiences.

   D They experience tension in their work.

9 What are we told about Rod Franks?

   A He used to be the director of a football club.

   B He switched from one career to another.

   C He used to be a professional trumpeter.

   D He disliked his original choice of career.

10 The LSO began playing abroad

   A only fairly recently.

   B over a hundred years ago.

   C when it was first set up.

   D when it needed money.

11 Orchestras have to travel abroad

   A to play with foreign conductors.

   B to record with foreign companies.

   C to make themselves better known.

   D to record with new solo players.

12 What does 'It' in line 30 refer to?

   A organising a number of recordings

   B visiting the most important markets

   C the expense of touring in a country

   D providing more than just concerts

13 Sue Mallet's arrangements for the LSO can be

   A affected by external circumstances.

   B made difficult by awkward players.

   C spoilt by overlooking tiny details.

   D spoilt by very careless planning.

14 What does the phrase 'with scientific accuracy' (line 36) suggest about Sue Mallet's planning?

   A It's very neat and tidy.

   B Her figures are correct.

   C She used to be a scientist.

   D The details are excellent.

15 According to the writer, what made a certain moment 'unforgettable' (line 45)?

   A the fact that the orchestra stood up

   B an individual's appreciation

   C the enthusiastic applause

   D the fact that a message was in English

PART 3

You are going to read a newspaper article about long-distance medical treatment. Seven sentences have been removed from the article. Choose from the sentences **A-H** the one which fits each gap **(16-21)**. There is one extra sentence which you do not need to use. There is an example at the beginning **(0)**.

Mark your answers **on the separate answer sheet**.

A However, a satellite phone, a computer and some simple technology could establish a direct link between them and hospital specialists.

B The new prescription is sent automatically to your home.

C Today it includes video technology and high-speed communications using satellites.

D In one recent case an oil-rig worker had a worsening headache two days after a head injury.

E It can help reduce queues and waiting times for doctors in hospitals.

F This means that students and teachers can share in live classes, which is a great improvement on traditional textbooks.

G This can save lives when bad weather makes it impossible to fly home someone who is ill and needs to go to hospital.

H Many elderly people who live alone may suddenly fall ill or have an accident at home.

Telemedicine

Telemedicine, the practice of medicine at a distance, began with the telephone. **0** **C**

A doctor in London can now examine a patient in the Middle East or South America. Three of the four Antarctic survey research bases now have computers, allowing transfer of medical information. **16**

Although telemedicine occurs in outer space, it will also change everyday medical practice on earth. **17** In addition, it can reduce the number of journeys a person might need to make to hospital for follow-up treatment and change the treatment of the elderly. **18** In cases like these, telemedicine could make doctors and nurses aware of who needs help and use a 'video visit' to reduce the cost of a home visit or an unnecessary trip to hospital.

Before too long you may be able to pick up the phone for a 'video-conferencing call' and talk to a doctor for advice. Your spots may then be 'examined' by a doctor fifty kilometres away using this video link.

Whereas most people in the developed world can easily visit a doctor or a hospital for a medical check, people in some developing countries are not so lucky. **19** For example, a young Swazi boy in South Africa suffering from an eye disease was 'examined' by doctors in London who were then able to decide what kind of treatment the boy needed.

Telemedicine could also change medical education by bringing the expert skills of the world's leading specialists to students throughout the world. Students in Africa or India can now watch a surgeon performing an operation in Europe or the US. There is already a medical education link between a university in the UK and a university in the Middle East. **20**

Ships and off-shore installations like drilling platforms are also making increasing use of telemedicine. **21** Stormy weather prevented him from being taken to the mainland, but a video discussion and examination by a doctor on land established that he was not at serious risk.

PART 4

You are going to read a magazine article about five people who were interviewed about going on holiday. For Questions **22-35**, choose from the people **(A-E)**. The people may be chosen more than once. When more than one answer is required, these may be given in any order. There is an example at the beginning **(0)**.

Mark your answers **on the separate answer sheet**.

Which of the questions refers to which person?

Who went away with a relative? | 0 | A |

Who learnt how to deal with a local custom? | 22 | |

Who found the atmosphere reduced their usual anxieties? | 23 | |

Who found the places rather mysterious? | 24 | |
                                                                  | 25 | |

Who got most pleasure from another person? | 26 | |

Who felt as if they were interfering in people's lives? | 27 | |

Who was surprised by the comfortable conditions? | 28 | |

Who found other people spoilt their holiday? | 29 | |

Who found their holiday experiences disturbing? | 30 | |
                                                                  | 31 | |

Who thought they had seldom had a better holiday? | 32 | |

Who appears interested in the history of the place? | 33 | |

Who hadn't planned their holiday? | 34 | |

Who chose a holiday to find out more about themselves? | 35 | |

Holidays

Many people go away on holiday and discover as much about themselves as they do about the places they visit.

A Hugo

When my eldest daughter, Alice, was ten, she asked for a holiday with me – just the two of us. I have four children so it can be difficult for Alice to get a word in, and I understood what she wanted. I decided to show her Venice, because it has such warm associations for me. I first went there with my wife shortly after we were married, and Alice was curious to see it.

We arrived at night, which was completely magical. The water gives the city a sense of mystery. Even if you've been down a street before, the next time you find it you see something different and that stops you recognising it. So you constantly get lost.

Alice loved Venice. We laughed a lot, and the best thing for me was seeing her excited face.

B Maria

I love deserts. I usually travel on my own and with more camera equipment than clothes. I've been to deserts all over the world but my favourite is the Sahara. During my last trip I went to Timbuctoo, which is an amazing place. Centuries ago it was at the centre of the trans-Saharan caravan routes, routes used by travellers and traders who rode their camels for weeks on end across the Sahara, north to south and east to west. There was even a university there. Today it's a strange place, rather like a ghost town.

There are tribesmen called Tuaregs who ride through the town on camels, very proud-looking men wearing blue robes, but although the local inhabitants are very friendly, I felt curiously out of place. It might have been to do with the fact that there were no other travellers or tourists there. I felt almost as if I should not be there, as if I was an intruder, and the last thing I felt able to do was to take photographs. People's lives seemed so private.

C Krystyna

I thought I would try an activity holiday last year as I enjoy the outdoor life. I usually end up lying on a beach somewhere but I reckoned an activity holiday would help me discover hidden talents, skills that I never knew I possessed. Perhaps I would turn out to be a brilliant canoeist, mountain climber or skydiver.

The trouble with holidays like this is that you may not like what you discover. I had forgotten that I would be with a group of people each day. It had never occurred to me how competitive some people would be. Whatever we did, they had to be first. First to put up their tent, first to reach the top of the mountain, fastest cyclist, and so on. They will also have the loudest voices and make the most irritating remarks. Such daily companions can come as a bit of a shock if you are more used to quiet conversations with your best friend.

D Robin

We arranged to go on safari, staying in one of those extraordinary hotels in the middle of nowhere in Africa. Our room was luxurious, with hot and cold running water and a fridge. At night we went out on a lake and when we got back to shore, a row of lantern lights led back to the main lodge. Then you sat in front of a huge fire and the guides told stories.

Part of the holiday included a canoe safari on the Zambezi river. In our canoe there was just my friend and myself and the guide. I'm not terribly athletic and when I got into the canoe I managed to tip it over and we all ended up in the water. I was quite frightened because of the crocodiles there. We couldn't turn the canoe upright but the guide was very calm. He pointed to a rock in the middle of the river and told us to swim to it as fast as we could, while he went to get help. Then he came back with another canoe, but after that I refused to go back on the water. I was quite surprised by my reaction. Not that I'd thought of myself as a particularly brave person, but the shock of what happened left me feeling very nervous.

E Daniel

I made a decision at the last minute to go to Jamaica. I booked a package holiday with a friend which included accommodation in a cottage and all our meals. We had so much fun – it was one of the best holidays I've ever had.

There are amazing sunsets in Jamaica and you can sit on the rocks and watch the sun go down. Everyone and everything is very relaxed. The thing you hear most often is 'No problem, man'. At first I thought they were just saying it, but then you realise nothing is a problem because the whole place is so relaxed. And that attitude makes you relax and forget about all the things you usually worry about.

We spent one day at a port watching a cruise ship come in. When that happens, all the shops double their prices and you have to bargain for anything you want to buy. You look at something and shake your head and they lower the price and you still shake your head, but you eventually find out at what stage you should agree a price. I bought some really great wooden statues for half the original price!

PART 1

You **must** answer this question.

1 You have just completed a coach tour which was very unsatisfactory. You decide to write to the coach company to complain about the tour and ask for your money back.

Read the advertisement carefully, including the comments which you have made. Using this information, write a letter to the company. You may include other relevant details of your own.

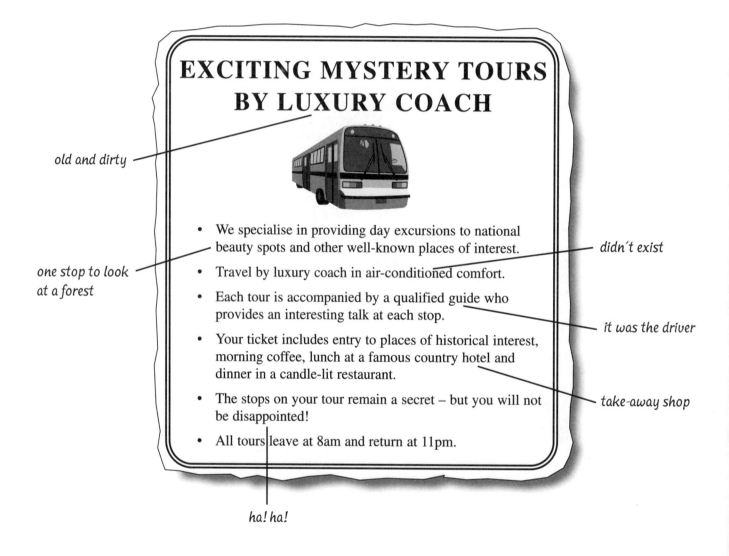

old and dirty

EXCITING MYSTERY TOURS BY LUXURY COACH

one stop to look at a forest

didn't exist

- We specialise in providing day excursions to national beauty spots and other well-known places of interest.
- Travel by luxury coach in air-conditioned comfort.
- Each tour is accompanied by a qualified guide who provides an interesting talk at each stop.

it was the driver

- Your ticket includes entry to places of historical interest, morning coffee, lunch at a famous country hotel and dinner in a candle-lit restaurant.
- The stops on your tour remain a secret – but you will not be disappointed!

take-away shop

- All tours leave at 8am and return at 11pm.

ha! ha!

Write a **letter** of between **120 and 180** words in an appropriate style.
Do not write any addresses.

PART 2

Write an answer to **one** of the Questions **2-5** in this part. Write your answer in **120-180** words in an appropriate style, putting the question number in the box.

2   Your local newspaper is going to include a weekly article in English for people who are interested in improving their knowledge of the language. You have been asked to write the first article, which must give suggestions on the ways in which people can help themselves when learning English.

   Write your **article**.

3   You have planned a holiday with an English-speaking friend, but last-minute difficulties mean that you you have to cancel the arrangements. Write to your friend explaining what has happened.

   Write your **letter**.

4   You have been reading a newspaper article about the number of people who consider shopping to be their main interest or hobby. Your teacher now wants to know your views on the following statement:

   Shopping can never be a serious hobby – it is just a waste of time.

   Write your **composition**.

5   **Background reading texts**

   Answer **one** of the following two questions based on your reading of **one** of the set books. Your answer should contain enough detail to make it clear to someone who may not have read the book. Write the letter **(a)** or **(b)** as well as the number **5** in the question box, and the **title** of the book next to the box.

   Either   **(a)**   'The storyline is always more important than the characters.' Is this true of the book or the short story which you have read?

   Or   **(b)**   If you had to choose a scene to illustrate the cover of the book which you have read, which scene would you choose and why?

PAPER 3   Use of English

PART 1

For Questions **1-15**, read the text below and decide which answer **A**, **B**, **C** or **D** best fits each space. There is an example at the beginning **(0)**.

Mark your answers **on the separate answer sheet**.

Example:

0	**A** makes	**B** suggests	**C** puts	**D** gives

0	A ⎵	B ▬	C ⎵	D ⎵

SCENTS IN THE OFFICE

The word *jasmine* **(0)** ..... images of a delicate white flower with a wonderful perfume. Many people believe that the flower's perfume has the **(1)** ..... to heal, and studies are being **(2)** ..... out on the effects of this and other perfumes in an office **(3)** ..... .

Researchers in Japan have found that **(4)** ..... the air was scented with jasmine, computer operators made 33% **(5)** ..... errors. Orange, rose and lavender perfumes have also been **(6)** ..... to make people work more efficiently and **(7)** ..... their stress levels.

(8) ..... these studies originally took place in Japan, a recent **(9)** ..... in the UK found that 40% of employers **(10)** ..... the idea of scenting the workplace. In fact, one store has already **(11)** ..... two different perfumes into the front and the back of its shop in the hope that they will **(12)** ..... a calming effect on its customers.

In the future, it is possible that public areas like banks will use their own particular perfume. In this way certain smells will **(13)** ..... themselves in a customer's mind with a particular **(14)** ..... . But not everyone is happy with this kind of development, as not **(15)** ..... is known about the long-term effect of breathing in these chemicals.

1	**A** way	**B** power	**C** control	**D** influence
2	**A** taken	**B** helped	**C** given	**D** carried
3	**A** surround	**B** area	**C** place	**D** environment
4	**A** when	**B** as	**C** for	**D** since
5	**A** less	**B** smaller	**C** fewer	**D** little
6	**A** arranged	**B** shown	**C** seen	**D** established
7	**A** lose	**B** reduce	**C** shrink	**D** weaken
8	**A** For	**B** Because	**C** Despite	**D** Although
9	**A** survey	**B** view	**C** examination	**D** account
10	**A** hold	**B** support	**C** provide	**D** consider
11	**A** put	**B** started	**C** introduced	**D** set
12	**A** build	**B** make	**C** have	**D** form
13	**A** join	**B** identify	**C** prove	**D** compare
14	**A** produce	**B** project	**C** process	**D** product
15	**A** enough	**B** all	**C** plenty	**D** insufficient

PART 2

For questions **16-30**, read the text below and think of the word which best fits each space. Use only **one** word in each space. There is an example at the beginning **(0)**.

Write your answers **on the separate answer sheet**.

Example: | **0** | *has* |

LONDON'S RIVER

The role of the River Thames **(0)** .... been of vital importance to London's history. **(16)** .... the city's beginnings as a Roman Empire trading post and military base, the Thames has connected London **(17)** .... the wider world beyond. **(18)** .... the height of the Industrial Revolution in the nineteenth century, the London docks were **(19)** .... of merchant ships; London was **(20)** .... biggest port in the world with hundreds of ships **(21)** .... to and from all five continents.

Today, **(22)** .... of that river traffic has disappeared, but the empty docklands are bursting back into life. **(23)** .... place of the old buildings with their smashed windows and broken roofs are homes, offices, riverside walks and the tallest building in Britain, known **(24)** .... Canary Wharf. Miles of new and improved roads have also been built, as **(25)** .... as an ultra-modern airport **(26)** .... is only a five-minute walk away from the nearest railway station.

In the sixteenth century, the king kept his hunting dogs on the flat marshy area beside the Thames, which is **(27)** .... it came to be **(28)** .... the Isle of Dogs. Today, the Isle of Dogs is **(29)** .... a space-age city, with a new railway travelling high **(30)** .... street level past exciting modern architecture.

PART 3

For Questions **31-40**, complete the second sentence so that it has a similar meaning to the first sentence, using the word given. **Do not change the word given.** You must use between two and five words, including the word given. Here is an example **(0)**.

Example:

0   The suitcase is not light enough for me to carry.

too

The suitcase .... for me to carry.

The gap can be filled by the words 'is too heavy' so you write:

0	is too heavy

Write **only** the missing words **on the separate answer sheet**.

---

31   The doctor examined my broken leg.

examined

My .... the doctor.

32   'Shall we go to the cinema?' said Maisie.

suggested

Maisie .... the cinema.

33   It isn't necessary to reserve a seat on the train.

need

You .... a seat on the train.

34   Could you close the window, please?

mind

Would .... the window, please?

35   There is no point in waiting for the bus.

worth

It .... for the bus.

36   Jo has stopped drinking coffee.

up

Jo .... coffee.

37   I last saw Jean two months ago.

for

I .... two months.

38   Amy's parents did not allow her to stay out late at night.

let

Amy's parents .... out late at night.

39   Despite being very tired, the old man carried on walking.

even

The old man carried on walking .... very tired.

40   If you don't feel well by tomorrow, you should see a doctor.

unless

You should see a doctor .... by tomorrow.

PART 4

For Questions **41-55**, read the text below and look carefully at each line. Some of the lines are correct, and some have a word which should not be there.
If a line is correct, put a tick (✓) by the number **on the separate answer sheet**. If a line has a word which should not be there, write the word **on the separate answer sheet**. There are two examples at the beginning **(0 and 00)**.

Examples:

0	✓
00	the

NOISE

0	Repetitive noise, day after day, can lead to stress and make life
00	miserable, especially for those with the health problems.
41	There is evidence that people are becoming more concerned
42	about noise. There are a number of more possible reasons for
43	this. People have the different reactions to noise. While many of us
44	have more time to take up leisure activities and interests, we don't
45	always stop to think about the effect of our activities are having on
46	others. However, the only problem isn't always one of insensitive
47	behaviour. Even homes that are so well built may be affected by
48	powerful modern stereo systems. What is music to one person's
49	ears could well be 'a terrible noise' to a neighbour and give to them
50	sleepless nights. Some noise is unavoidable, and when it comes
51	to the everyday sounds of a busy neighbourhood, people have some
52	different lifestyles, different tastes and different levels of tolerance.
53	A barking dog may not disturb much one person but it can slowly
54	drive another person crazy. If we all do liked the same sounds at the
55	same time, life would be so much simpler.

PART 5

For Questions **56-65**, read the text below. Use the word given in capitals at the end of each line to form a word that fits in the space in the same line. There is an example at the beginning **(0)**.

Write your answers **on the separate answer sheet**.

Example: | 0 | *operation* |

INTERNATIONAL PEN FRIEND CLUB

International Pen Friends (IPF) started off as a small **(0)** *operation* in 1967.   **OPERATE**

The organisation now has 300,000 members in 210 countries **(56)** ..... ; its   **WORLD**

youngest member is eight and its oldest is 93. IPF **(57)** ..... come from   **APPLY**

all walks of life to join this guaranteed pen friend **(58)** ..... . Members are   **SERVE**

given a list of fourteen names and addresses for **(59)** ..... with people   **CORRESPOND**

around the world.

Exchanging letters is an **(60)** ..... to learn more about geography,   **OPPORTUNE**

travel and foreign languages. And once the **(61)** ..... has developed, people   **FRIEND**

can explore the **(62)** ..... of exchange holidays. Because letter writing is   **POSSIBLE**

very **(63)** ..... , some relationships are bound to develop, although IPF is   **PERSON**

anxious that the club is not seen as a **(64)** ..... bureau but simply a   **MARRY**

(65) ..... way of meeting people.   **DIFFER**

PAPER 4 Listening

PART 1

You will hear people talking in eight different situations. For Questions **1-8**, choose the best answer, **A**, **B** or **C**.

---

1   You are being shown around a factory.

What is the speaker talking about?

A   wood

B   diamonds   [| 1]

C   steel

2   Listen to this boy talking.

Why is he upset?

A   He lost his wallet.

B   He missed his train.   [| 2]

C   He bought the wrong ticket.

3   Listen to these students discussing a party they've been to.

What did they think of it?

A   It was very noisy.

B   It was very boring.   [| 3]

C   It was very crowded.

4   You overhear a man talking to a customer in a shop.

What is he suggesting?

A   The customer should try another shop.

B   One of the new coats might suit her.   [| 4]

C   Last season's colours were nicer.

5 Listen to a photographer talking about some pictures she's taken.

What does she say about the results?

A The colours are far too bright.

B The prints are not light enough.

C The photos are disappointing.

| | 5 |

6 You hear a mother talking to her child.

What has he done?

A lost his jumper

B broken his leg

C hurt his knee

| | 6 |

7 Your friend is using your phone.

Who is she speaking to?

A a doctor's receptionist

B a hospital receptionist

C a dental receptionist

| | 7 |

8 You hear two people talking about a journey.

What is the problem?

A There are no trains.

B The roads are very busy.

C The bus drivers are on strike.

| | 8 |

PART 2

You will hear a radio interview with a young man called Iain, who has just spent a year in Russia. For Questions **9-18**, complete the sentences.

9   Iain spent [_____ **9**] in St Petersburg.

10   Students joined the orientation programme from [_____ **10**] .

11   Even in August, Omsk was [_____ **11**] .

12   He went to Novosibirsk on a [_____ **12**] .

13 + Novosibirsk is a [_____ **13**] and [_____ **14**] city.
14

15   Iain spent two hours daily [_____ **15**] .

16   A teacher encouraged him to give [_____ **16**] to earn some money.

17   He couldn't cook without [_____ **17**] from his mother.

18   Iain held [_____ **18**] to improve his students' English.

PART 3

You will hear five different people talking about jobs. For Questions **19-23**, choose from the list **A-F** the job each speaker is describing. Use the letters only once. There is one extra letter which you do not need to use.

A	singer	
		Speaker 1 **19**
B	disco owner	
		Speaker 2 **20**
C	farmer	
		Speaker 3 **21**
D	teacher	
		Speaker 4 **22**
E	artist	
		Speaker 5 **23**
F	restaurant owner	

PART 4

You will hear a conversation between a hotel owner, a tour operator and a guest.

Answer Questions **24-30**, by writing **H** (for hotel owner)

T (for tour operator) or

G (for guest) in the boxes provided.

24   Who sounds rather impatient at first?   24

25   Who feels apologetic about the situation?   25

26   Who thinks the problem is someone else's responsibility?   26

27   Who offers to contact another hotel?   27

28   Who says the opposite of what they mean?   28

29   Who makes a definite promise?   29

30   Who says the hut might be rather uncomfortable?   30

PAPER 5   The Speaking Test

PART 1   (3 MINUTES)

The teacher (interlocutor) invites each candidate to speak in turn and give personal information about themselves.

Candidates can expect a variety of questions, some of which will require short answers, and some requiring longer answers about their present circumstances, past experiences and their future plans, such as:

Where are you from?

Have you always lived there / here?

What about your family? Can you tell us something about your family?

Do you work or are you studying?

What subject(s) are you studying? / What does your work involve?

What kind of job do you hope to do in the future?

Candidates talk to each other and the interlocutor.

PART 2   (4 MINUTES)

Teacher   Now I'm going to give each of you two different photographs. I'd like you both to show each other your pictures and then talk about them.

You each have a minute for this part, so don't worry if I interrupt you.

X, here are your two pictures. Let **Y** have a look at them. They are both photographs of people in different places.

*(Show photos 1 and 2 to **X**.)*

Y, I'll show you your photos in a minute.

Now **X**, I'd like you to compare and contrast your photos and talk about the way these people are spending their free time.

Remember, you have about a minute for this.

*(Allow about a minute for **X** to talk without interruption.)*

Thank you. **Y**, which of these activities would you prefer to do?

*(Allow **Y** about 20 seconds.)*

Thank you. Now **Y**, here are your photographs. Let **X** have a look at them. They both show people wearing special clothes.

*(Show photos 3 and 4 to **Y**.)*

Now **Y**, I'd like you to compare and contrast your photos and say why you think these people are dressed like this.

Remember, you have about a minute for this.

*(Allow about a minute for **Y** to talk without interruption.)*

Thank you. Now **X**, would you be interested in seeing anything like this?

*(Allow **X** about 20 seconds.)*

Thank you.

PART 3   (3 MINUTES)

Teacher   I want you to imagine that a new leisure centre is opening in your area. Here is a picture of some of the things which the planners might include.

*(Show picture 5 to **X** and **Y**.)*

I want you to talk to each other and decide which **5** things you think are the most suitable and why.

You have about three minutes to talk to each other, so don't worry if I stop you.

*(Allow **X** and **Y** about 3 minutes.)*

Thank you.

PART 4   (4 MINUTES)

Teacher   Do you think it's important for a town to have a leisure centre? Why? / Why not?

Do you think it's possible for a leisure centre to provide facilities for different ages or is it likely to attract just young people?

If money is limited, what kind of facilities are the most important?

Do you think leisure centres will become more or less important in the future? Why? / Why not?

Do you think such facilities should be free of charge to the people who live in the area?

Thank you. That is the end.

Practice Test 4

PAPER 1   Reading

1 hour 15 minutes

PART 1

You are going to read a magazine article about an artificial language called Esperanto which was invented in 1887. Choose the most suitable summary sentence from the list **A-I** for each part **(1-7)** of the article. There is one extra heading which you do not need to use. There is an example at the beginning **(0)**.

Mark your answers **on the separate answer sheet**.

A	People doubt the advantages of Esperanto.
B	Esperanto can be a threat.
C	National politics is more important than communication.
D	Learning Esperanto is not as hard as learning some languages.
E	Little use is made of Esperanto.
F	People disagree over language and identity.
G	Esperanto is certain to succeed in future.
H	Requests to develop Esperanto are ignored.
I	Some people think English has too much influence.

Whatever happened to Esperanto?

0	E

At a recent Esperanto conference there were about 2,000 people from 65 to 70 different countries present. They had no language problem and there was not an interpreter in sight! If the worldwide, scattered community of Esperanto speakers could come together like this, without a language problem, why is Esperanto not more widely used?

1	

It is not that as a means of communication it is inadequate. Esperanto has probably more richness than most national languages. Its educational, scientific and cultural value was recognised by UNESCO* as early as 1954. Since then UNESCO has twice made a plea for European member states to encourage the teaching of Esperanto. No one has taken it up.

2	

There are a few reasons why the obvious merits of Esperanto have not been used. Language is tied up with the question of national pride and power. The idea of a language that is inter- or non-national not belonging to any particular tribe or nation, but available to everyone, creates enthusiasm in some, and concern, uncertainty and suspicion in others.

3	

Governments, by their nature, are more concerned with their short-term political agendas than solving the world's language problems. They see their first duty to their own people, not to foreigners.

4	

In the world of today, it is the English-speaking peoples and their governments that have world political power and they do not see any major language problem. Rather, they believe that English is winning. Those who do recognise the problem lack that kind of power. In between the two are those who are ambitious and hope that their language will become more important.

5	

The sociological and political history of Esperanto throws a great light on this. During its 110-year history it has been both forbidden to teach Esperanto in certain countries and discouraged in others. Many Esperantists have experienced prejudice and imprisonment or even been killed. The idea of internationalism, with people being able to talk and correspond with foreigners, can be seen as a dangerous thing in times of national crisis. It suggests lack of loyalty or patriotism.

6	

Esperanto belongs to no one and yet to everyone. In more tolerant times and countries, governments tend to take no interest in Esperanto, the probabilities being that many of their citizens will not even hear of its existence. When they do hear of it, the probabilities again are that many will decide against learning it because it is not seen as producing any economic or financial benefit. The field is left to the idealists.

7	

What is the best, the fairest and most efficient solution, not only for preserving existing languages and cultures but also for making communication easier? Of the many attempts made over the years to find that solution, only Esperanto has survived the test of time. There are some who say Esperanto is not perfect. However, the basic truth is that it works, with the learning time to become fluent in Esperanto being approximately a fifth of that required for an English speaker to learn French, and perhaps a twentieth of the time required to learn Russian or Japanese.

*United Nations Educational, Scientific and Cultural Organisation

PART 2

You are going to read an article about taking part in the Olympic Games by Bryn Vaile, who won a gold medal for sailing in 1988. For Questions **8-14**, choose the answer (**A**, **B**, **C** or **D**) which you think fits best according to the text.

Mark your answers **on the separate answer sheet.**

The moment for Olympic glory and gold occurs once every four years – a moment which becomes the focus for the lives of athletes from all over the world. This one event is their ultimate goal, the high point of their ambition, and in order to achieve their dream they are prepared to make any sacrifice.

Most athletes consider themselves fortunate to have one chance to shine at an Olympic Games, while others may be fortunate to get two or more chances. All are selected by their national Olympic Committee to represent their country, and once selected they face two major demands. The first is the mountain of form filling, paperwork and administration. The second is to finalise their preparation for the Games. Most athletes have highly-developed training schedules which enable them to reach the height of their performance for a particular event. However, the Olympics creates its own timetable and pressures.

When I was selected to represent Great Britain, I had approximately a hundred days to prepare. This included finalising training plans, raising nearly £16,000 towards the costs, seeing to travel arrangements and entry forms, and having discussions with my employer about extra time off work to allow me to prepare fully.

Throughout my sailing career I had never had the opportunity to become a full-time athlete, so I needed to pursue my business career at the same time as my sporting objectives. However, any top-class athlete in any sport needs a level of business skills when competing at Olympic standard. They need the ability to plan and arrange for all the expenses effectively as well as work towards definite aims.

Once you arrive, you stay in the Olympic 'Village', which is really a small town housing 15,000 people – 10,000 athletes and 5,000 officials – from every imaginable culture and background. It is fascinating to watch athletes from tiny gymnasts to huge weightlifters and basketball players, and best of all is the excitement at being part of such a select gathering. There are training facilities, souvenir shops, launderettes, a bank and post office, as well as the Village restaurant which seats over 3,000 at one time. The outdoor plazas become a meeting place for athletes from around the world, and from there you can see people returning with their medals proudly displayed around their necks or bravely hiding their tears of defeat or disappointment.

So what does it feel like to go to an Olympics? It can be summed up in many ways by the opening ceremony, where thousands of athletes and officials parade wearing their team kit. To most it is an event they will never forget and the honour of just being there is almost magical. And perhaps winning a medal is one of life's major experiences. For me it was the thoughts of family and friends who had all played a part on my road to success, and it felt wonderful.

8 According to the writer, in addition to the physical routines, taking part in the Olympics also means
   A organising all the necessary paperwork.
   B giving up one's job for a short period of time.
   C getting others to help with the administration.
   D sacrificing one's free time during the preparation.

9 In preparation for the Olympics, athletes' training programmes are
   A organised by their personal trainers.
   B governed by their national committee.
   C designed to avoid too much individual stress.
   D affected by the stress of the occasion itself.

10 What does 'This' in line 23 refer to?
   A having been selected to compete
   B the time available for preparation
   C the need to raise a sum of money
   D planning arrangements at work

11 Anyone who reaches the Olympics will benefit from having
   A their costs paid by their employer.
   B their expenses professionally handled.
   C a background in the business world.
   D a full-time job in the sporting world.

12 What did the writer enjoy most about staying in the Olympic Village?
   A the size of the village
   B the range of competitors
   C the sense of belonging
   D the variety of nationalities

13 What does the writer say about competitors who were unsuccessful?
   A They clearly showed how extremely upset they were.
   B They felt that taking part was more important than winning.
   C They did not mind other people offering them sympathy.
   D They did their best to keep their feelings to themselves.

14 How did the writer react when he won a medal?
   A He thought of all the support he had received.
   B He realised it would never happen again.
   C He knew it was a very important moment.
   D He felt it was the greatest honour of his life.

PART 3

You are going to read a newspaper article about a woman who liked adventure. Seven sentences have been removed from the article. Choose from the sentences **A-H** the one which fits each gap **(15-20)**. There is one extra sentence which you do not need to use. There is an example at the beginning **(0)**.

Mark your answers **on the separate answer sheet.**

A In 1926 she married a racing driver and started driving cars herself.

B On another occasion she is afraid the engine will fail and so she decides to make an emergency landing in the sand.

C She found time to write five books, including her autobiography, and at the age of 78 she drove at 110 miles per hour around a racing circuit.

D He replied that it would, and within a week she was flying solo.

E She remarked that the only chance she had to have her hair cut was by making crash-landings.

F Immediately after qualifiying she took off on a 16,500-mile flight around the world, crossing 23 countries on three continents.

G After she had completed her trip round the world she made a record in which she talks about her various experiences in her tiny plane, sometimes even facing death.

H When she was a child, her horse galloped away without warning.

Never Mind the Dress, How Much is that Plane?

Mary Bruce was shopping one day in one of the most expensive streets in London. She was looking for a nice new dress, when instead she noticed a showroom with a small light aircraft for sale at a fairly reasonable price. She went away to try on a dress. It did not suit her. The plane did. She asked the man in the shop whether the plane would take her round the world. **0** | **D**

That day in 1930 Mary Bruce was 35 years old and it was the beginning of an adventure for a very brave woman who became the most inexperienced pilot ever to fly round the world. She qualified for her pilot's licence in the minimum forty hours' flying time at the local airport near her home in the same year. **15**

Mary Bruce had faced danger on other occasions and loved anything that was risky and frightening. She was one of the first women to buy a motorcycle, and was always being taken to court for speeding down country lanes. **16** As a couple they once drove as far as they could into the Arctic Circle before they ran out of road. In 1927, encouraged by her husband, she won a race for women drivers in the Monte Carlo rally, and two years later she was the first person to set a distance record for driving a powerboat.

17 In one instance she talks about how she has seen land, but as the plane's oil pressure was zero she wonders whether she will be able to stay up in the air long enough to reach it. **18** No one listening to the recording could fail to be impressed by her bravery and sense of adventure.

One of her few complaints was that she attracted so much interest whenever she made an arranged stopover. **19** That kind of remark was typical of her attitude, and it was hardly surprising that she drew crowds of people wherever she landed.

In 1933 she successfully completed one of the world's first mid-air refuelling operations and in 1939 she won prizes in a showjumping event on her horse. Even in old age she did not slow down. **20** She died in 1990 at the age of 94.

PART 4

You are going to read about six different books for 8- to 12-year-old children. For Questions **21-33**, choose from the book titles **(A-F)**. The titles may be chosen more than once. When more than one answer is required, these may be given in any order. There is an example at the beginning **(0)**. For Questions **34** and **35**, choose the answer **(A, B, C** or **D)** which you think fits best according to the text.

Mark your answers **on the separate answer sheet**.

Which of the books

has pictures in it?	**0**	**B**
deals with teenagers being frightened by others?	**21**	
	22	
	23	
contains more than one story?	**24**	
seems to be the least successful?	**25**	
describes a difficult but entertaining relationship?	**26**	
might make the reader feel rather depressed?	**27**	
contains more than one style of writing?	**28**	
is very amusing?	**29**	
	30	
is rather hard for this age group?	**31**	
brings together the present world and the past?	**32**	
	33	

34 Where would you expect to find this text?
   A in a children's magazine
   B in a school handbook
   C in a bookseller's catalogue
   D in a school advertisement

35 Why would someone read this text?
   A to help them choose a book for a child
   B to find out who won the award for best writer
   C to find out about books for young adults
   D to see who the readers' favourite writer is

Grown-up Books for Smart Children

Writers of fiction for eight- to twelve-year-olds seem to fall into two groups. Some writers imitate the voices of children and others write in their own voices, clearly and with something new to say. On the whole, the latter are funnier and more original.

A A Handful of Gold

A Handful of Gold by Joan Aiken demonstrates that a writer doesn't have to spell things incorrectly or put on silly voices to be funny. This book is a selection of Aiken's stories written over the past forty years. Although the stories contain humour, many of them end sadly. In *A Serial Garden*, for example, a boy walks into a garden drawn on the back of a cereal packet and almost manages to make an old man lastingly happy. But at the final moment fate prevents this from happening and the reader is left gasping with the sense of loss. The writing is full of imaginative power and this book is a treasure for any 10-year-old.

B The Wreck of the Zanzibar

The Wreck of the Zanzibar by Michael Morpurgo is a story which contains an extract from a diary by Great Aunt Laura written in 1907 on her fourteenth birthday – although the book is suitable for younger readers. Laura's story describes life in a fishing community which is struggling to survive; its style is simple, direct and moving with beautiful drawings.

C Red, White and Blue

Red White and Blue by Robert Leeson deals with the theme of bullying. The pages in the book are edged in white, red and blue to copy the notepaper which young Gawain uses for his homework, his diary and his own fantasy story. Gawain is thirteen and in his first year at secondary school. He is bullied by older boys at school, his teenage brother also treats him unkindly and his father went missing during a war before Gawain was born. The author makes good use of three different styles, and it is a very likeable book.

D The Trokeville Way

Bullying also occurs in *The Trokeville Way* by Russell Hoban. This book deserves attention because it is more ambitious than most for this age group. It sets out to do something difficult: to express the troubles and gradual awareness of adolescence through one boy's experience of a dream world. Sadly, it is not entirely successful. The book has moments of beautiful writing, but it is also difficult to follow at times and repetitive, although a sophisticated twelve-year-old might enjoy the demands it makes on the reader.

E Granny the Pag

More successful is the book by Nina Bawden called *Granny the Pag*. This book's great strength is its wonderful central character, twelve-year-old Catriona's amazing grandmother. She wears old dresses, smokes constantly and rides a motorbike. She embarrasses her granddaughter but at the same time she is a perfect companion. Catriona lives with her because of her parents' careers in a television soap opera. The book is touching, true and funny, and the author shows how it is possible to write for children without having to sound like a child.

F The Pits

The Pits by Lesley Howarth is a very successful book. The storyteller is the ghost of a Stone Age man who lived thousands of years ago. He has picked up the modern way of speaking of the world he now inhabits and uses this language to describe his adventures. The contrast between the tone he uses and the content of his adventures creates great comedy. It also gives the writer the opportunity to discuss all sorts of modern issues like gangs, drunkenness, family life and even bullying.

PAPER 2   Writing

PART 1

You **must** answer this question.

1   You are on the social committee at your college and you are in charge of the arrangements for the end-of-term disco. You have booked the DJ (disc jockey) for 7.45pm as he needs time to set up his equipment. Unfortunately, the hall is not available between 5.45pm and 8.45pm.

Look carefully at the notice about the disco and your notes. Then write a letter to the manager of the disco, Ed Brown, using the relevant information. Explain the problem, apologise for the inconvenience and suggest an alternative arrangement.

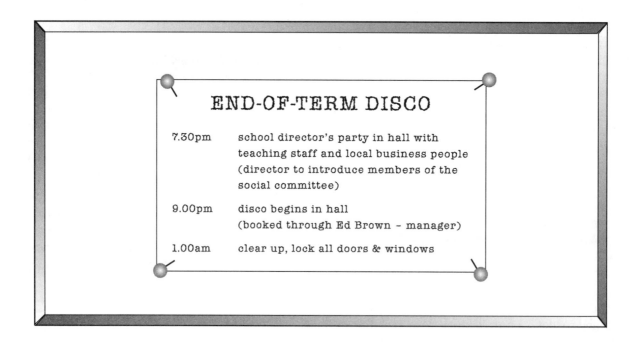

END-OF-TERM DISCO

7.30pm	school director's party in hall with teaching staff and local business people (director to introduce members of the social committee)
9.00pm	disco begins in hall (booked through Ed Brown – manager)
1.00am	clear up, lock all doors & windows

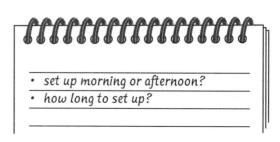

- set up morning or afternoon?
- how long to set up?

Write a **letter** of between **120 and 180** words in an appropriate style.
Do not write any addresses.

PART 2

Write an answer to **one** of the Questions **2-5** in this part. Write your answer in **120-180** words in an appropriate style, putting the question number in the box.

2   Your teacher has asked you to write on the following topic for your school newspaper:

We should not expect to drive a car if we want a safe and healthy environment.

Write your **composition**.

3   You are going to enter a short-story competition organised by a foreign-language magazine. You have to write a story which begins with the words:

I woke up hoping that the postman would bring the letter I was waiting for.

Write your **story**.

4   Your teacher has asked you to write about the day trip which your class made to one of the main attractions in your area; what you write will be included in the school newspaper.

Write your **account**.

5   **Background reading texts**

Answer **one** of the following two questions based on your reading of **one** of the set books. Your answer should contain enough detail to make it clear to someone who may not have read the book. Write the letter **(a)** or **(b)** as well as the number **5** in the question box, and the **title** of the book next to the box.

Either   **(a)**   If you could meet one of the characters from the book you have read, who would you choose and why?

Or   **(b)**   Choose one of the incidents from the book you have read and explain why it has stayed in your memory.

PAPER 3   Use of English

PART 1

For Questions **1-15**, read the text below and decide which answer **A**, **B**, **C** or **D** best fits each space. There is an example at the beginning **(0)**.

Mark your answers **on the separate answer sheet**.

Example:

0   **A**   kinds   **B**   means   **C**   ways   **D**   methods

0	A	B	C	D

THE LIQUORICE PLANT

Liquorice has been used in various **(0)** ..... for thousands of years. Centuries ago the Chinese praised it for its healing **(1)** ..... , and in ancient Greece doctors found the liquorice root **(2)** ..... relief from chest complaints. It is claimed that Roman soldiers were given liquorice root to chew, as a means of **(3)** ..... their thirst on long marches.

The liquorice plant looks like a small bush with pale blue flowers. **(4)** ..... , it is the root which is all important, for it is from the root that the juice is extracted to **(5)** ..... what we know as liquorice. The roots are soft and flexible and **(6)** ..... glycyrrhizin, which is one of the sweetest **(7)** ..... known to man, and is fifty times sweeter **(8)** ..... sugar. The roots take four years to grow **(9)** ..... , and by that time can be up to ten metres long.

Liquorice harvesting has changed little over the **(10)** ..... . In the autumn, the plants are lifted and the upper parts are thrown **(11)** ..... . The roots are then sorted, piled up and left to dry. After nine or ten months, when only 10% of the **(12)** ..... remains, the roots are pressed into large **(13)** ..... and taken to factories where the juice is extracted. This extracted liquid is **(14)** ..... into a golden brown powder, and it is this **(15)** ..... material which is used in today's sweet-making industry.

1	**A**	forms	**B**	standards	**C**	cures	**D**	qualities
2	**A**	provided	**B**	was	**C**	made	**D**	bought
3	**A**	filling	**B**	satisfying	**C**	improving	**D**	cooling
4	**A**	Because	**B**	Since	**C**	However	**D**	Also
5	**A**	give	**B**	shape	**C**	form	**D**	have
6	**A**	hold	**B**	contain	**C**	construct	**D**	raise
7	**A**	substances	**B**	materials	**C**	features	**D**	solids
8	**A**	then	**B**	more	**C**	as	**D**	than
9	**A**	fully	**B**	widely	**C**	occasionally	**D**	gradually
10	**A**	times	**B**	centuries	**C**	periods	**D**	seasons
11	**A**	off	**B**	away	**C**	over	**D**	out
12	**A**	moisture	**B**	damp	**C**	water	**D**	drops
13	**A**	stocks	**B**	stores	**C**	bundles	**D**	collections
14	**A**	drawn	**B**	poured	**C**	removed	**D**	dried
15	**A**	fresh	**B**	raw	**C**	original	**D**	uncooked

PART 2

For questions **16-30**, read the text below and think of the word which best fits each space. Use only **one** word in each space. There is an example at the beginning **(0)**.

Write your answers **on the separate answer sheet**.

Example: | **0** | *what* |

WEATHER FORECASTING

All sorts of people need to know **(0)** .... the weather is going to do, but they do **(16)** .... all need to know the same things for the same period of time. If you're sailing a small boat for a day, it's only a **(17)** .... hours that matter. If you're a water company worrying about water supplies, you want to know the chances of rain over **(18)** .... next six months.

(19) .... getting the forecast right matters to so many people, the weather business is always at the forefront of technology. **(20)** .... is a weather satellite **(21)** .... flies from pole to pole every hour and **(22)** .... quarter, covering the whole globe every day **(23)** .... reporting back to Earth from fifty miles up. Others 20,000 miles up are moving at the same relative speed **(24)** .... the Earth below them **(25)** .... that they can keep a continuous watch on different parts of the world.

Weather forecasting **(26)** .... on processing and reporting an enormous **(27)** .... of detailed observations from around the world within minutes, so meteorologists **(28)** .... among the leading users of really massive computers. But there's still no replacement **(29)** .... the experienced human forecaster **(30)** .... it comes to knowing what the local weather is doing.

PART 3

For Questions **31-40**, complete the second sentence so that it has a similar meaning to the first sentence, using the word given. **Do not change the word given.** You must use between two and five words, including the word given. Here is an example **(0)**.

Example:

0   The suitcase is not light enough for me to carry.

too

The suitcase .... for me to carry.

The gap can be filled by the words 'is too heavy' so you write:

0	is too heavy

Write **only** the missing words **on the separate answer sheet**.

---

31   In 2001 my parents will celebrate twenty-five years of marriage.

been

By 2001 my parents .... for twenty-five years.

32   As I had my camera with me, I was able to take lots of photos.

not

If I had not had my camera with me, I .... to take lots of photos.

33   Farmers in the US grow a large proportion of the world's wheat.

is

A large proportion of the world's wheat .... farmers in the US.

34   My car is being repaired tomorrow.

having

I'm .... tomorrow.

35 I'm sorry you didn't get the job you applied for.

wish

I .... the job you applied for.

36 Thieves broke into the gallery and stole three paintings.

with

Thieves broke into the gallery .... three paintings.

37 The lecturer was so boring that everyone was asleep by the end.

off

The lecturer was so boring that everyone .... by the end.

38 Greg should be here in time for lunch.

supposed

Greg .... here in time for lunch.

39 Take an umbrella with you in case it rains.

because

Take an umbrella with you .... rain.

40 'Why don't you stop work for a few hours?' Mario said to his wife.

break

Mario suggested .... from her work for a few hours.

PART 4

For Questions **41-55**, read the text below and look carefully at each line. Some of the lines are correct, and some have a word which should not be there.
If a line is correct, put a tick (✓) by the number **on the separate answer sheet**. If a line has a word which should not be there, write the word **on the separate answer sheet**. There are two examples at the beginning **(0)** and **(00)**.

Examples:

0	✓
00	the

CRETE

0   I first visited Crete in 1973 on a study tour with a famous archaeologist.

00   Since then I have returned each year at the every oppportunity. I am

41   attracted to the history, the climate, the food and wine, and the wonderful

42   scenery, and I would very much like to live there permanently if possible.

43   This year I have been so lucky enough to get a job as a tour guide, which

44   means I can spend almost six months on to the island. I will be involved in

45   organising and planning tours for which groups of tourists interested in

46   getting on to know the island and the people. The groups are quite small,

47   usually a maximum of twelve people, so the atmosphere is relaxed and informal.

48   A typical day's itinerary usually includes time for having a swim and a

49   leisurely lunch, as well as opportunities for exploring on the foot. Although

50   each day will be based on a minibus trip, I think it's very important to

51   be able to stop wherever and whenever people want. Sometimes people

52   just want to admire the scenery or have a coffee, and it's too important that

53   they should not feel rushed when they're on holiday. I am really very

54   looking forward to the experience. It feels that as if I will be on holiday myself

55   for a few months instead of working for my living.

PART 5

For Questions **56-65**, read the text below. Use the word given in capitals at the end of each line to form a word that fits in the space in the same line. There is an example at the beginning **(0)**.

Write your answers **on the separate answer sheet**.

Example:

0	rapidly

THE END OF THE ROAD FOR WALKING

Walking is **(0)** ...*rapidly*... becoming a thing of the past according to a   **RAPID**

recent report. It warns of serious health and **(56)** ..... problems if   **ENVIRONMENT**

the **(57)** ..... continues, since walking as a means of transport has   **TEND**

gone down by a **(58)** ..... in the last twenty years.   **FIVE**

The report blames the increased use of cars for doing the **(59)** .....   **SHOP**

and taking children to school. This has created **(60)** ..... pollution   **ATMOSPHERE**

as well as an **(61)** ..... environment for walking in. If the recent decline   **ATTRACT**

is maintained, walking will become **(62)** ..... and we will not be   **NEED**

walking anywhere by 2025. Although this may seem an **(63)** ..... ,   **EXAGGERATE**

the **(64)** ..... of the car is greater than ever, and young people   **POPULAR**

cannot wait to become car **(65)** ..... themselves.   **OWN**

PAPER 4   Listening

PART 1

You will hear people talking in eight different situations. For Questions **1-8**, choose the best answer, **A**, **B** or **C**.

---

1   You hear a hotel guest complaining to the manager of the hotel.

What is he complaining about?

   A   the phone in his room

   B   the TV in his room   `1`

   C   the safe in his room

2   You hear a woman asking about her missing glasses.

Where does she think she left them?

   A   with some magazines

   B   in her hand luggage   `2`

   C   on her aircraft seat

3   You overhear two students discussing some arrangements.

What is the problem?

   A   The concert has been cancelled.

   B   The trip to the coast is too expensive.   `3`

   C   Two events are on the same day.

4   Listen to this radio announcement.

What is the warning about?

   A   damaged bridges

   B   violent weather   `4`

   C   delayed departures

5   Listen to this tour guide talking to some people.

Where are they going?

A   on a mountain tour

B   on an island tour

C   on a factory tour

| | 5 |

6   Listen to these two girls talking about a road accident.

What happened to Linda?

A   She ran into a line of parked cars.

B   She was knocked down by a car.

C   She fell over right in front of a taxi.

| | 6 |

7   You hear a man talking.

What is he talking about?

A   finding a lot of money

B   counting a lot of money

C   winning a lot of money

| | 7 |

8   Listen to this brother and sister talking together.

What are they discussing?

A   a present for a sick relative

B   a special birthday present

C   a present for an anniversary

| | 8 |

PART 2

You will hear a man who has just flown in from abroad being interviewed about the airport's facilities. For Questions **9-18**, complete the notes.

9	Passenger returning from:	**9**
10	Main purpose for visit abroad:	**10**
11	Method of transport to reach airport:	**11**
12	Preferred form of public transport:	**12**
13	Check-in: time spent in queue:	**13**
14	Baggage reclaim: time spent waiting:	**14**
15 + 16	Type of refreshment facilities required:	**15**
		16
17 + 18	Shops visited:	**17**
		18

PART 3

You will hear five different people talking about things they miss. For Questions **19-23**, choose from the list **A-F** the thing each person misses. Use the letters only once. There is one extra letter which you do not need to use.

A   a pet animal

Speaker 1   [ ] **19**

B   human contact

Speaker 2   [ ] **20**

C   having energy

Speaker 3   [ ] **21**

D   a sense of space

Speaker 4   [ ] **22**

E   a life of luxury

Speaker 5   [ ] **23**

F   a particular food

PART 4

You will hear a conversation between Isabella and Gavin, who run a small restaurant. For Questions **24-30**, decide which of the statements are true and which are false, by writing **T** for true or **F** for false in the boxes provided.

24   Isabella is uncertain about employing extra staff. | | **24**

25   Gavin feels he is under pressure at work. | | **25**

26   Isabella thinks they should only serve dinners. | | **26**

27   They agree about raising the restaurant prices. | | **27**

28   Gavin is enthusiastic about changing the lunch menu. | | **28**

29   Isabella thinks hot food would be a good idea. | | **29**

30   They decide on a standard charge for lunch. | | **30**

PAPER 5   The Speaking Test

PART 1   (3 MINUTES)

The teacher (interlocutor) invites each candidate to speak in turn and give personal information about themselves.

Candidates can expect a variety of questions, some of which will require short answers, and some requiring longer answers about their present circumstances, past experiences and their future plans, such as:

Where do you come from?

Can you tell me something about your family?

How do you normally spend your holidays?

What did you do for your last holiday?

Where would you most like to go for a future holiday?

How important will English be for you in the future?

Candidates talk to each other and the interlocutor.

PART 2   (4 MINUTES)

Teacher   Now I'm going to give each of you two different photographs. I'd like you both to show each other your pictures and then talk about them.

You each have a minute for this part, so don't worry if I interrupt you.

X, here are your two pictures. Let **Y** have a look at them. They are both photographs of parents and children.

*(Show photos 1 and 2 to **X**.)*

Y, I'll show you your photos in a minute.

Now **X**, I'd like you to compare and contrast your photos and talk about the things that parents and children enjoy doing together.

Remember, you have about a minute for this.

*(Allow about a minute for **X** to talk without interruption.)*

Thank you. **Y**, what did you enjoy doing with your family when you were younger?

*(Allow **Y** about 20 seconds.)*

Thank you. Now **Y**, here are your photographs. Let **X** have a look at them. They both show stalls in markets.

*(Show photos 3 and 4 to **Y**.)*

Now **Y**, I'd like you to compare and contrast your photos and say what impressions you have of these different markets.

Remember, you have about a minute for this.

*(Allow about a minute for **Y** to talk without interruption.)*

Thank you. Now **X**, which of these two markets would you enjoy wandering around and why?

*(Allow **X** about 20 seconds.)*

Thank you.

PART 3   (3 MINUTES)

Teacher   I want you to imagine that you have to choose some pictures which are going to be used to encourage people to visit different museums and exhibition centres.
*(Show picture 5 to **X** and **Y**.)*

I want you to talk to each other and decide which **3** pictures you think would be the most suitable and why.

You have about three minutes to talk to each other, so don't worry if I stop you.
*(Allow **X** and **Y** about 3 minutes.)*

Thank you.

PART 4   (4 MINUTES)

Teacher   Do you think it's a good idea to have museums and exhibition centres where you can touch things instead of just looking at them? Why? / Why not?

Did you enjoy visiting museums when you were a child or did your parents have to drag you there? Why? / Why not?

Do you have a favourite museum? Why? / Why not?

Do you think children can learn more from watching television than visiting a museum? Why? / Why not?

What are the ways in which we can learn and have fun at the same time?

Thank you. That is the end.

Practice Test 5

1 hour 15 minutes

PART 1

You are going to read a magazine article about a holiday organisation called *Earthwatch*. Choose the most suitable heading from the list **A-I** for each part **(1-7)** of the article. There is one extra heading which you do not need to use. There is an example at the beginning **(0)**.

Mark your answers **on the separate answer sheet**.

A	The value of personal and financial investment
B	Reacting to unsatisfactory projects
C	How to join a project
D	A different kind of holiday
E	Getting to a destination
F	*Earthwatch* still attracting criticism
G	The purpose in establishing *Earthwatch*
H	Hardship part of the fun
I	Transferring one's abilities to a different environment

Worlds of Difference

Max Le Grand investigates a very different kind of tourism.

0	D

If you are not attracted to the kind of holiday where you spend your time with hundreds of other tourists on crowded beaches, then you might be interested in finding out about an alternative kind of holiday. There is an increasing interest in what is called eco-tourism, which appeals to people who are concerned about the environment. A few popular tour operators offer holidays to faraway places where tourists can watch wildlife in their natural surroundings, for example, but there are also organisations which offer holidays where people actually work in local conditions on various projects.

1	

One such organisation is called *Earthwatch*, which was set up as a charity to support important scientific, environmental and cultural research through involving members of the public. Over the past 25 years, some 40,000 people have taken part in *Earthwatch* projects on a voluntary basis, and 65% of those people have been happy to roll up their sleeves and get down to work.

2	

However, you won't find *Earthwatch* holidays on sale through your local travel agent. In the first instance you have to find out what projects *Earthwatch* are involved in. You can do this by contacting the organisation direct or by buying their catalogue, which provides information on over 140 scientific projects throughout the world. You then decide which project you would like to be involved in. Following that you are given further information before you finally decide you would like to be included in a particular project.

3	

Earthwatch does not ask for any qualifications; people are required to apply their everyday work skills in a situation where they work as members of a small research group. People must be able to live together, sometimes in very basic conditions, to pursue a job which can last from one week to a month. The point of *Earthwatch* is to learn the skills associated with professional expedition research like mapping, photographing, gathering data and making collections of plants.

4	

Everyone who takes part in a trip has to pay their own costs. Consequently, most people put as much as they can into working on a project to get their money's worth even though they are on holiday. But if you happen to work in an office or a factory, such a holiday is really exciting. The fact that you might suffer a bit of discomfort because of the heat or the cold, living in a tent or sleeping under a palm tree, is all part of the adventure. Besides, some people actually enjoy the simplicity of getting back to basics.

5	

As people come from all over the world to join the various projects, you do not necessarily fly out with other volunteers. You generally travel independently to a country and make your way to a common meeting point at a hotel in the city. Once the group has met, some form of overland transport will take you to the exact location where you will be working. It might be hundreds of miles away in a very remote area, in which case there could be some trekking or horse-riding to arrive at the project base camp.

6	

In extreme cases, people may find that they do not enjoy the experience and they want to leave the project. If *Earthwatch* feels they have matched a person to the wrong project, they will be able to help that individual find another job to suit his or her temperament. There are projects in 55 countries around the world, and not all of them are in distant or faraway regions. Some people are happy to work in rainforests in Ecuador, or in the Sahara desert, whereas other people prefer to work in Europe.

7	

Organisations like *Earthwatch* have not been free from objections. There have been concerns that 'tourists' may be taking away jobs from local people or that it is a way of getting cheap labour. Neither of these objections is true. Basically, *Earthwatch* brings together groups of adventurous people who want to help solve some of the world's problems and who are prepared to pay out of their own pocket for the opportunity to do so.

PART 2

You are going to read a magazine article about a woman who helps business executives to improve their image. For Questions **8-15**, choose the answer (**A**, **B**, **C** or **D**) which you think fits best according to the text.

Mark your answers **on the separate answer sheet**.

Maura Fay is a casting agent. She chooses actors for films, advertisements and soap operas, and her life is filled with people who refer to each other as 'darling' and kiss the air when they meet. It is not an environment which is immediately attractive to serious business people. Yet Maura Fay is now finding that her new courses, which are intended to improve nervous executives' presentation techniques, are being taken very seriously indeed.

'It began,' says Ms Fay, 'about four years ago during one of the workshops I set up for actors. Not stars, but those who could take on small, character parts. Teenagers especially, or people in their fifties and sixties who might have talent, but have no idea of how to present themselves in front of an audience. That's when it struck me, in the middle of one of these sessions. I suddenly thought, this is what the business community needs.'

For Ms Fay it was obvious. Business people are trained to do business, not to perform. Yet if they are to put across their ideas, their knowledge and their information in a memorable way, they need to understand actors' techniques. So Maura Fay set about teaching business people how to win and influence their audiences, how to handle nerves, how to control their breathing and how to make a good impression. It took a long time but the outcome was worth it.

'Most of our trainers are drama teachers. Many have been actors, some still are. In every workshop we do, we involve professional actors. So you can be taught by someone you've seen on television the night before. It's all very exciting and part of new management thinking as we approach the next century. Technology has changed the face of offices throughout the world, but companies are people, not things, after all.'

Some business communities are rather cautious about accepting Maura Fay's techniques. Meanwhile other organisations are working along similar lines and using theatre-based workshops not only for putting across business ideas, but also for dealing with people's behaviour. Theatrical workshops, like music, can cross language and cultural frontiers. Different nationalities will interpret things in different ways, but that is one reason why a theatrical workshop is so interesting and useful.

Maura Fay is also concerned with how to do business in different cultures and she employs actors from various countries to help with multi-cultural workshops. These actors then demonstrate exactly how clients in their own countries would behave in certain business situations, and that is very valuable experience for companies looking to do business in a particular country.

line 16

8 How have business people's attitudes changed towards Maura Fay?
  A They no longer take her seriously.
  B They are more attracted to the theatre.
  C They think she is a very good agent.
  D They value what she can offer them.

9 What does 'it' in line 16 refer to?
  A choosing young stars for new films
  B advertising her existing courses
  C developing ideas for businesses
  D setting up business courses for actors

10 Maura Fay's original workshops were intended to
  A improve star performers' abilities.
  B give ordinary actors more skills.
  C help actors get better jobs.
  D turn young people into stars.

11 What did Maura Fay think business people most needed?
  A more knowledge of the theatre
  B learning to remember information
  C understanding how to relax
  D an awareness of acting skills

12 How does Maura Fay feel about her business courses?
  A They're very hard work.
  B They're very up to date.
  C They're very impersonal.
  D They're very dramatic.

13 What does the writer say about theatre-based workshops?
  A Some people are not very keen on them.
  B They influence people's treatment of others.
  C They mean people interpret things wrongly.
  D Some people find them rather uninteresting.

14 Maura Fay employs actors from other countries who
  A discuss people's business plans.
  B explain their own business ideas.
  C act out 'foreign' business reactions.
  D teach business people how to behave.

15 What is the writer's purpose in the text?
  A to complain about new business training methods
  B to help drama teachers change their profession
  C to provide information about training people
  D to argue that actors are good at business

PART 3

You are going to read a newspaper article about tourism. Eight sentences have been removed from the article. Choose from the sentences **A-I** the one which fits each gap **(16-22)**. There is one extra sentence which you do not need to use. There is an example at the beginning **(0)**.

Mark your answers **on the separate answer sheet**.

A For example, Bhutan, sandwiched between India and China, charges visitors $250 a day, which increases income and reduces numbers.

B There is a limit to the amount of deserted beach which any island can offer; the unspoilt gets spoilt as hotels and casinos are built, golf courses mapped out, and roads constructed through areas of natural beauty.

C Moreover, for many countries in the developing world, tourism is an ideal source of job creation and wealth, if managed properly.

D Tourists will not go to places which are polluted and where the landscape has been lost.

E The Mediterranean, which attracts 120 million tourists a year, is known as one of the dirtiest seas in the world.

F Yet it was an Englishman, Thomas Cook, who founded the travel agency which still bears his name and organised the first of many package holidays in 1841.

G By the year 2010 the number of tourists travelling internationally is expected to double to more than a billion a year.

H But the chances of finding new unspoilt destinations is low, especially as growing numbers of people expect to travel.

I Much of this is due to the enormous increase in tourism amoung countries in the region as average incomes have risen.

Wish you weren't here

From the Antarctic to Lapland, from Siberia to the Amazon rainforest, there are few places in the world which are untouched by tourism. For those who want to get away from other people and the pressure of everyday life, it is becoming increasingly difficult to find privacy. Complaints about the impact and the numbers and behaviour of tourists are nothing new. As long ago as 1870 an English clergyman and diarist complained about British tourists being offensive. **0 F**

Until 1915 most European states did not require travellers to carry a passport for entry. But that changed with the growth of travel, which increased after the Second World War. In 1950 there were 25 million tourists according to the World Tourism Organisation; in 1995 more than 561 million tourists visited other countries. **16**

Holiday destinations which are far away from the mass-market package holiday destinations are considered by many people to convey a social status. Your position in society is higher if you can take your holiday on an island which has remained undeveloped, for example, well away from other people. But as more people follow, such an island becomes increasingly less attractive. **17**

There is also the psychological side, in which upmarket travellers grow to dislike a resort because it is no longer reserved for people like themselves. So as the most popular destinations become 'ruined', more people are looking for distant and unspoilt destinations. **18**

The countries of east Asia and the Pacific rim have seen the fastest growth in the number of foreign tourists visiting them over the past decade. **19**

There is little doubt that tourism can bring enormous economic benefits to countries. In some countries it may be the single biggest earner of that country's income and the biggest employer. **20**

However, the balance between running tourism at a profit but not at the expense of natural resources has begun to concern everyone in the industry. The authorities in many of the world's developing destinations are becoming better at managing the environmental impact of their foreign visitors. **21**

This limitation reduces the bad effects on the environment and maintains its attraction for the well-off travellers. This balance is important because a tourist destination depends on the attractiveness of its physical surroundings.

22 The end of the environment is the end of tourism.

PART 4

You are going to read a magazine article about some young people in the UK. For Questions **23-35**, choose from the young people **(A-E)**. The people may be chosen more than once. When more than one answer is required, these may be given in any order. There is an example at the beginning **(0)**.

Mark your answers **on the separate answer sheet**.

Which of the questions refers to which young person?

Who dislikes history?	**0**	D
Who is allowed to stay out the latest?	**23**	
Who complains about a brother?	**24**	
Who expresses admiration for a parent?	**25**	
	26	
Who shares a sporting interest with a parent?	**27**	
Who is looking forward to having a family?	**28**	
	29	
Who is the most fashion conscious?	**30**	
Who hopes to spend time away without parents?	**31**	
Whose parents are annoyed by their child's habits?	**32**	
Who hasn't made new friends yet?	**33**	
Who regularly goes out with friends at weekends?	**34**	
	35	

Young Lives

Children are growing up faster than ever. What is it really like to be a young person today? Some young people talk openly and honestly about themselves.

A Simon (15)

I'm studying geography, maths and sciences, although I think I'd eventually like to do something with computers. I think if you know something about computing, it's much easier to get a job these days.

I spend a lot of time at home with my sister and my mum and dad. My father and I get on quite well and we watch a lot of sport together on TV, especially football. During the week I have piles of homework to do, but at weekends I'm allowed to stay out until 10 o'clock at night. I generally meet up with some of my schoolmates and we go into town to a cinema or a coffee bar.

I'm quite fussy about my clothes and the way my hair looks, so although my mum buys all my clothes, I tell her what to get me – like the right jeans and trainers.

B Rosie (14)

I watch about an hour's television every day and we watch videos a lot, too. I love action films, horrors and comedy. At weekends I go swimming with people from my class and if I get bored in the evenings, I read and draw.

I really respect my mother, who has done a great deal for us as my father is in the army and away from home for long periods of time. On weekdays I'm allowed to stay out until 9 o'clock and at weekends until 11.

Every year we all go on holiday, my parents and my two younger brothers. We usually rent a cottage somewhere abroad and close to the sea. We went to France last year and that was brilliant and I actually got to use my French when I had to ask for ice-cream and things. I think when I'm a bit older, I'd like to go on holiday with my friends although I suppose I'd expect my parents to pay for it!

C Ewan (16)

I'm sport mad. Football, basketball, gymnastics, cricket. I'd love to make a living from sport. My parents get really fed up with me because I tend to plan my homework around what's on television.

I don't have much free time because of all the sport and training I do, although occasionally I might go to a party at a weekend with some of my older friends. I think my parents give me enough freedom, but I've never really asked to stay out late or overnight because I'm always up early to do my sports training.

I think marriage is very important. That's what I see myself doing: getting an education, a job and then settling down, getting married and having children.

I don't have much time for politicians as all they seem to do is argue, and I think they put their personal interest before the good of the country because they want to get to the top.

D Mira (12)

At school I like maths, science and sports, but I hate history – and we get far too much homework each night.

The best thing about school is breaktimes because I can play with my friends. The teachers are a bit strict and tell you off for talking and things. But one of them is all right and she lets us do more or less what we want so I like her.

When I'm not at school I like to play outside with my friends or watch television. I don't know many people around here as we've just moved, but we've got a much bigger garden where I can play with my brother. My brother is really horrible: he draws all over the posters on my bedroom wall and gets me into trouble with my mum.

When I grow up, I want to be a fashion designer and model. I think you're grown up when you get to twenty because then you can stay up late.

I love holidays. This year we went to Greece where it was amazingly hot and I made lots of new friends. I'd like to go to Spain or Egypt next year.

E Frances (14)

When I'm not at school I like to play football with my brothers and I also like watching football on television.

My best friend lives opposite and we get on really well together. We're allowed to go out until 9 o'clock each evening but usually we stay in each other's room chatting. She and I are about the same size so we share our clothes.

The person I would most like to grow up like is my mother because she's done so much and lived in lots of different countries. She's creative, intelligent and talented, and she gets things done for herself.

One day I suppose I'll have a husband and children, which will be great, and I really want a car.

And I want to travel as well and be able to go on holidays abroad.

PAPER 2   Writing

PART 1

You **must** answer this question.

1   The director of your college has asked you to write a letter to a group of foreign teachers who will be spending the day at the college. The teachers have made various requests but it will not be possible for them to do everything they ask.

Read carefully the part of the letter from the organiser of the teachers' visit and the notes which the college director has made. Then write a letter explaining what decisions have been made about the arrangements for their visit and add any other necessary points.

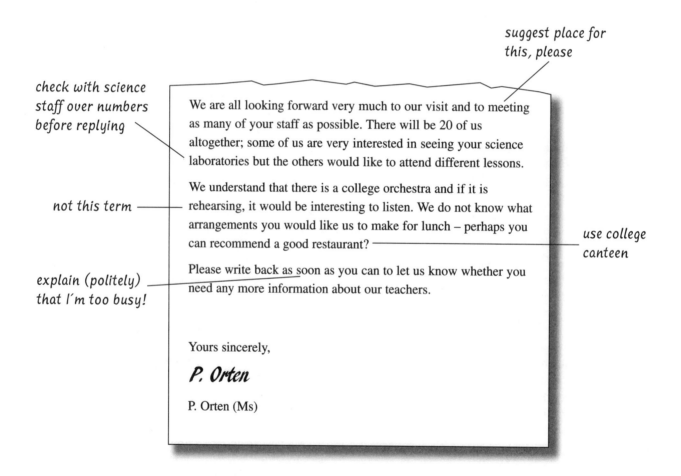

suggest place for this, please

check with science staff over numbers before replying

We are all looking forward very much to our visit and to meeting as many of your staff as possible. There will be 20 of us altogether; some of us are very interested in seeing your science laboratories but the others would like to attend different lessons.

not this term

We understand that there is a college orchestra and if it is rehearsing, it would be interesting to listen. We do not know what arrangements you would like us to make for lunch – perhaps you can recommend a good restaurant?

use college canteen

explain (politely) that I'm too busy!

Please write back as soon as you can to let us know whether you need any more information about our teachers.

Yours sincerely,

P. Orten

P. Orten (Ms)

Write a **letter** of between **120 and 180** words in an appropriate style.
Do not write any addresses.

PART 2

Write an answer to **one** of the Questions **2-5** in this part. Write your answer in **120-180** words in an appropriate style, putting the question number in the box.

2 If you had to choose one favourite place to visit, where would it be and why would you choose it?

Write your **composition**.

3 Your friend is recovering from an operation and has been feeling rather depressed. Write a letter suggesting something you could both do which would cheer him/her up.

Write your **letter**.

4 You have been asked for your views on whether the supermarkets in your area should stay open for twenty-four hours a day, seven days a week. Your local newspaper will publish the best piece of writing in its English-language section.

Write your **article**.

5 **Background reading texts**

Answer **one** of the following two questions based on your reading of **one** of the set books. Your answer should contain enough detail to make it clear to someone who may not have read the book. Write the letter **(a)** or **(b)** as well as the number **5** in the question box, and the **title** of the book next to the box.

Either **(a)** 'For a book to be enjoyable it should have a happy ending.' Briefly say if you agree or disagree with this statement, and whether or not the book which you have read supports your views.

Or **(b)** Who is your favourite character and who is your least favourite character in the book you have read and why?

PAPER 3 Use of English

PART 1

For Questions **1-15**, read the text below and decide which answer **A**, **B**, **C** or **D** best fits each space. There is an example at the beginning **(0)**.

Mark your answers **on the separate answer sheet**.

Example:

0	**A** occasions	**B** times	**C** events	**D** days

0	**A**	**B**	**C**	**D**

LETTER WRITING

Because of national festivals such as Christmas or personal **(0)** ..... like birthdays, there is undoubted pleasure in waiting for a letter to **(1)** ..... through the letterbox.

People love receiving personal letters, but are not as **(2)** ..... on replying to them. A survey of letter writers in the UK **(3)** ..... that young people are among the most **(4)** ..... letter writers. They are even prepared to **(5)** ..... a correspondence with a pen friend they may never meet.

However, the survey also produced a strange **(6)** ..... . While 94% of people **(7)** ..... that a letter showed that someone had put time and thought into its **(8)** ..... , 69% said they would **(9)** ..... to spend their time on other things than writing. Overall, almost a third thought that receiving good **(10)** ..... was the best thing about receiving letters.

Not surprisingly, only 15% thought that postal communication would **(11)** ..... in the future. It is expected that the Internet and e-mail will make personal letter writing even **(12)** ..... , but the Post Office is looking at ways of giving technology a human **(13)** ..... . People at home will be able to send messages or letters electronically to a central processing centre. They will then be **(14)** ..... out and put into envelopes in the traditional way, so the postman will still have the job of **(15)** ..... the post.

1	**A** post	**B** enter	**C** drop	**D** push
2	**A** keen	**B** anxious	**C** eager	**D** concerned
3	**A** described	**B** meant	**C** showed	**D** made
4	**A** usual	**B** frequent	**C** busy	**D** often
5	**A** do	**B** begin	**C** hold	**D** write
6	**A** problem	**B** matter	**C** result	**D** decision
7	**A** shared	**B** wondered	**C** liked	**D** agreed
8	**A** content	**B** material	**C** substance	**D** argument
9	**A** rather	**B** consider	**C** prefer	**D** enjoy
10	**A** information	**B** facts	**C** news	**D** greetings
11	**A** raise	**B** increase	**C** swell	**D** gain
12	**A** lesser	**B** smaller	**C** lower	**D** rarer
13	**A** shape	**B** body	**C** face	**D** figure
14	**A** printed	**B** sent	**C** written	**D** developed
15	**A** serving	**B** finding	**C** delivering	**D** doing

PART 2

For Questions **16-30**, read the text below and think of the word which best fits each space. Use only **one** word in each space. There is an example at the beginning **(0)**.

Write your answers **on the separate answer sheet**.

Example: | **0** | *the* |

SHOPPING LIST OF THE FUTURE

Foods with special health effects are the big idea of **(0)** .... future. **(16)** .... is claimed that one milk drink will be able to protect people against cancer and another drink product will increase brain power. These foods, **(17)** .... as 'functional foods', are the result **(18)** .... increased scientific understanding of **(19)** .... makes a healthy diet.

One of the milk drink products, called Toptal, **(20)** .... marketed in packs of seven tiny bottles – one for **(21)** .... day of the week – and contains a thin brown liquid which is said to protect people against various diseases. **(22)** .... drink product, which stops tooth decay, is being sold in some countries **(23)** .... the answer to dental problems caused **(24)** .... sugary drinks. A member of the group of manufacturers involved in diet and health said: 'We are moving to the point **(25)** .... we can tell which elements of food have which effects. We **(26)** .... talking about a very different idea of food. **(27)** .... the commercial point of view, functional foods have **(28)** .... tremendous future.'

Although **(29)** .... is no question that these foods are beneficial, the extent to **(30)** .... they benefit health remains uncertain.

PART 3

For Questions **31-40**, complete the second sentence so that it has a similar meaning to the first sentence, using the word given. **Do not change the word given.** You must use between two and five words, including the word given. Here is an example **(0)**.

Example:

0   The suitcase is not light enough for me to carry.

too

The suitcase .... for me to carry.

The gap can be filled by the words 'is too heavy' so you write:

0	*is too heavy*

Write **only** the missing words **on the separate answer sheet**.

---

31   I lost my way because I didn't take a map.

had

If I .... , I wouldn't have lost my way.

32   Bill Gates is thought by many people to be among the richest men in the world.

that

Many people .... world's richest men is Bill Gates.

33   Our local supermarket employs over 200 people.

are

Over 200 people .... our local supermarket.

34   This coffee is too weak for me.

not

This coffee .... for me.

35   Have you any idea who owns this house?

house

Have you any idea .... is?

36   It's not my fault that the car was damaged.

blame

Don't .... being damaged.

37   Don is the only person I know who went to university.

other

I do .... than Don who went to university.

38   Although my parents don't have much money, they are very generous.

despite

My parents are very generous .... much money.

39   Mark has never been abroad before.

first

This is the .... abroad.

40   Carla is more interested in music than in sport.

as

Carla is not .... she is in music.

PART 4

For Questions **41-55**, read the text below and look carefully at each line. Some of the lines are correct, and some have a word which should not be there.

If a line is correct, put a tick (✓) by the number **on the separate answer sheet**. If a line has a word which should not be there, write the word **on the separate answer sheet**. There are two examples at the beginning **(0)** and **(00)**.

Examples:

0	✓
00	SO

LUCKY ESCAPE

0	I have always been nervous of flying, although I realise that statistics
00	show that it is so one of the safest ways of travelling. If I can take the
41	train, or better still drive, then I much too prefer to do so. When it comes
42	to long journeys, however, flying is usually unavoidable. I was recently
43	booked on a transatlantic flight, but on my way to the airport I was much
44	held up by heavy traffic on the motorway. As a result of, when I eventually
45	got to the airport, I discovered that I had missed my flight. At first I was
46	really worried that I would not to be able to catch another one, but as
47	I had an 'open ticket' I was simply booked onto the next available flight.
48	I settled down to wait for in the departure lounge and then heard an
49	announcement that a flight (the one which I have had missed, in fact)
50	would shortly be landing. Although there was no danger, the pilot was
51	experiencing engine trouble and so had decided to return back. You
52	can imagine my feelings of relief that I had not been on board. In the
53	event, everyone was transferred to a new plane, and so that I finally
54	ended up travelling on the flight which I had originally should have been
55	on – but had fortunately missed!

PART 5

For Questions **56-65**, read the text below. Use the word given in capitals at the end of each line to form a word that fits in the space in the same line. There is an example at the beginning **(0)**.

Write your answers **on the separate answer sheet**.

Example:	0	*recognition*

THE PARALYMPICS

The Paralympic Games continue to gain **(0)** *recognition* worldwide, and like   **RECOGNISE**

the Olympic Games they are held every four years. **(56)** ..... come from   **COMPETE**

all over the world to demonstrate their **(57)** ..... skills and to join in the   **SPORT**

celebration of their magnificent athletic **(58)** ..... .   **ACHIEVE**

The rise of the Paralympics led to the first fully **(59)** ..... 'parallel' games   **NATION**

in Seoul in 1988. They were enormously **(60)** ..... and were followed by   **SUCCESS**

an even bigger event in Barcelona in 1992. The **(61)** ..... and commitment   **DETERMINE**

shown by the parathletes has been very **(62)** ..... in finding sponsorship   **INFLUENCE**

and funding from organisations, **(63)** ..... bodies and private businesses. The   **GOVERN**

Paralympics have caught the public's **(64)** ..... and imagination and seem   **ATTEND**

set to reach even greater **(65)** ..... in the years to come.   **HIGH**

PAPER 4   Listening

PART 1

You will hear people talking in eight different situations. For Questions **1-8**, choose the best answer, **A**, **B** or **C**.

---

1   You hear a man explaining something to a child.

What is he talking about?

A   a gun
B   a telescope
C   a camera

	1

2   Listen to this person in a market.

What is he selling?

A   watches
B   phones
C   jewellery

	2

3   You hear two friends talking about a journey.

What happened?

A   The flight was very late.
B   The bus was cancelled.
C   The train was delayed.

	3

4   You have turned on your radio.

Where is this programme being broadcast from?

A   a concert hall
B   an open-air theatre
C   a football stadium

	4

5   Listen to this man talking to his colleague on the phone.

What does he want to borrow?

A   some keys

B   a programme

C   a computer

| | 5 |

6   You overhear a girl explaining how she got a concert ticket.

How did she feel at the time?

A   amazed

B   satisfied

C   grateful

| | 6 |

7   You hear a boy talking about a day out.

Where has he been?

A   an air show

B   a swimming pool

C   a museum

| | 7 |

8   Listen to a woman talking to a friend.

What does she want her friend to do?

A   iron some clothes

B   do the shopping

C   cook a meal

| | 8 |

PART 2

You will hear part of a radio programme about sleep. For Questions **9-18**, complete the notes.

---

9   Basic number of hours' sleep needed each night:

	9

10   Club has organised activity called:

	10

11   People sleep best in conditions where there is:

	11

12 + To sleep really well people need to feel:
13

	12	and

	13

14 + Cave has some particular disadvantages:
15 +
16 +
17

damp (but not cold)

	14

	15

	16

	17

18   Main fear for some people:

	18

PART 3

You will hear five different people talking about a famous film star. For Questions **19-23**, choose from the list **A-F** which of the opinions each speaker expresses. Use the letters only once. There is one extra letter which you do not need to use.

A   She is a moody person.

Speaker 1	19

B   She ignores criticism.

Speaker 2	20

C   She is quite secretive.

Speaker 3	21

D   She is well liked by foreign audiences.

Speaker 4	22

E   She enjoys attention.

Speaker 5	23

F   She is not very talented.

PART 4

You will hear a radio discussion about an arts festival. For questions **24-30** choose the best answer, **A**, **B** or **C**.

24 What did Roland Welsh feel about his trip before he went?

  A He was not keen on the idea.

  B He thought it sounded excellent. | 24 |

  C He had heard it was quite dull.

25 The weekend consisted of

  A getting free tickets for shows.

  B watching live entertainment. | 25 |

  C queuing for various shows.

26 What surprises the interviewer?

  A Tourists get free invitations.

  B People perform for nothing. | 26 |

  C Visitors buy cheap tickets.

27 Some events last

  A the whole evening.

  B over two hours. | 27 |

  C less than an hour.

28 What impressed Roland about the weekend?

  A the careful planning

  B the range of activities | 28 |

  C the original ideas

29 How was the city kept clean?

  A It was swept at the end of the day.

  B It was cleared at the end of the festival. | 29 |

  C It was cleaned throughout the day.

30 What is Roland's opinion of the weekend?

  A It must be expensive to run.

  B It's not something to do every year. | 30 |

  C It's very effective advertising.

PAPER 5   The Speaking Test

PART 1   (3 MINUTES)

The teacher (interlocutor) invites each candidate to speak in turn and give personal information about themselves.

Candidates can expect a variety of questions, some of which will require short answers, and some requiring longer answers about their present circumstances, past experiences and their future plans, such as:

Where are you from?

What are you studying? / What does your job involve?

How important is learning English for you?

What kind of music do you most enjoy listening to?

How interested are you in either playing or watching sport?

What do you want to do in the future?

Candidates talk to each other and the interlocutor.

PART 2   (4 MINUTES)

Teacher Now I'm going to give each of you two different photographs. I'd like you both to show each other your pictures and then talk about them.

You each have a minute for this part, so don't worry if I interrupt you.

X, here are your two pictures. Let **Y** have a look at them. They both show people enjoying themselves.

(Show photos 1 and 2 to X.)

Y, I'll show you your photos in a minute.

Now **X**, I'd like you to compare and contrast your photos and say what you think these people are doing to enjoy themselves.

Remember, you have about a minute for this.

(Allow about a minute for X to talk without interruption.)

Thank you. **Y**, which of these activities would you most enjoy?

(Allow Y about 20 seconds.)

Thank you. Now **Y**, here are your photographs. Let **X** have a look at them. They both show different places.

(Show photos 3 and 4 to Y.)

Now **Y**, I'd like you to compare and contrast your photos and say what you think are the advantages and disadvantages of living in the country.

Remember, you have about a minute for this.

(Allow about a minute for Y to talk without interruption.)

Thank you. Now **X**, would you rather live in a town or in the country?

(Allow X about 20 seconds.)

Thank you.

PART 3   (3 MINUTES)

Teacher   I want you to imagine that you are designing a leaflet to advertise an advice centre where people can go to talk about problems or anything that is worrying them.
(Show picture 5 to X and Y.)

I want you to talk to each other and decide which **3** pictures you think should be included and why.

You have about three minutes to talk to each other, so don't worry if I stop you.
(Allow X and Y about 3 minutes.)

Thank you.

PART 4   (4 MINUTES)

Teacher   Do you think this kind of service is useful? Why? / Why not?

Do you think people find it easier to talk to complete strangers about things that worry them? Why? / Why not?

Do you think your family and friends are the best people to ask for advice? Why? / Why not?

Do you think it's best to write to a problem page in a magazine or a newspaper if you need advice? Why? / Why not?

Do you think listening to people is more important than being able to offer advice? Why? / Why not?

Thank you. That is the end.

CAMBRIDGE
EXAMINATIONS, CERTIFICATES AND DIPLOMAS
ENGLISH AS A FOREIGN LANGUAGE

University of Cambridge
Local Examinations Syndicate
International Examinations

SAMPLE

For Supervisor's use only		
Shade here if the candidate is ABSENT or has WITHDRAWN		

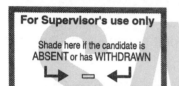

Examination Details 9999/01   99/D99

Examination Title First Certificate in English

Centre/Candidate No. AA999/9999

Candidate Name A.N. EXAMPLE

• Sign here if the details above are correct

☒

• Tell the Supervisor now if the details above
  are not correct

Candidate Answer Sheet: FCE Paper 1 Reading

Use a pencil

Mark ONE letter for each question.

For example, if you think **B** is the right answer to the question, mark your answer sheet like this:

| 0 | A B   D |

Change your answer like this:

| 0 | A   C D |

1	A B C D E F G H I
2	A B C D E F G H I
3	A B C D E F G H I
4	A B C D E F G H I
5	A B C D E F G H I

6	A B C D E F G H I
7	A B C D E F G H I
8	A B C D E F G H I
9	A B C D E F G H I
10	A B C D E F G H I
11	A B C D E F G H I
12	A B C D E F G H I
13	A B C D E F G H I
14	A B C D E F G H I
15	A B C D E F G H I
16	A B C D E F G H I
17	A B C D E F G H I
18	A B C D E F G H I
19	A B C D E F G H I
20	A B C D E F G H I

21	A B C D E F G H I
22	A B C D E F G H I
23	A B C D E F G H I
24	A B C D E F G H I
25	A B C D E F G H I
26	A B C D E F G H I
27	A B C D E F G H I
28	A B C D E F G H I
29	A B C D E F G H I
30	A B C D E F G H I
31	A B C D E F G H I
32	A B C D E F G H I
33	A B C D E F G H I
34	A B C D E F G H I
35	A B C D E F G H I

CAMBRIDGE
EXAMINATIONS, CERTIFICATES AND DIPLOMAS
ENGLISH AS A FOREIGN LANGUAGE

University of Cambridge
Local Examinations Syndicate
International Examinations

For Supervisor's use only

Shade here if the candidate is
ABSENT or has WITHDRAWN

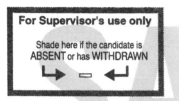

☒

Examination Details	9999/03	99/D99
Examination Title	First Certificate in English	
Centre/Candidate No.	AA999/9999	
Candidate Name	A.N. EXAMPLE	

• Sign here if the details above are correct

• Tell the Supervisor now if the details above
  are not correct

Candidate Answer Sheet: FCE Paper 3 Use of English

Use a pencil

For **Part 1**: Mark ONE letter for each question.

For example, if you think **C** is the
right answer to the question,
mark your answer sheet like this:

0	A B C

For **Parts 2, 3, 4** and **5**: Write your
answers in the spaces next to the
numbers like this:

0	

Part 1				
1	A	B	C	D
2	A	B	C	D
3	A	B	C	D
4	A	B	C	D
5	A	B	C	D
6	A	B	C	D
7	A	B	C	D
8	A	B	C	D
9	A	B	C	D
10	A	B	C	D
11	A	B	C	D
12	A	B	C	D
13	A	B	C	D
14	A	B	C	D
15	A	B	C	D

Part 2	Do not write here
16	16
17	17
18	18
19	19
20	20
21	21
22	22
23	23
24	24
25	25
26	26
27	27
28	28
29	29
30	30

Turn
over
for
Parts
3 - 5
→

Part 3		Do not write here		
31		31 0 ▭	1 ▭	2 ▭
32		32 0 ▭	1 ▭	2 ▭
33		33 0 ▭	1 ▭	2 ▭
34		34 0 ▭	1 ▭	2 ▭
35		35 0 ▭	1 ▭	2 ▭
36		36 0 ▭	1 ▭	2 ▭
37		37 0 ▭	1 ▭	2 ▭
38		38 0 ▭	1 ▭	2 ▭
39		39 0 ▭	1 ▭	2 ▭
40		40 0 ▭	1 ▭	2 ▭

Part 4		Do not write here
41		▭ 41 ▭
42		▭ 42 ▭
43		▭ 43 ▭
44		▭ 44 ▭
45		▭ 45 ▭
46		▭ 46 ▭
47		▭ 47 ▭
48		▭ 48 ▭
49		▭ 49 ▭
50		▭ 50 ▭
51		▭ 51 ▭
52		▭ 52 ▭
53		▭ 53 ▭
54		▭ 54 ▭
55		▭ 55 ▭

Part 5		Do not write here
56		▭ 56 ▭
57		▭ 57 ▭
58		▭ 58 ▭
59		▭ 59 ▭
60		▭ 60 ▭
61		▭ 61 ▭
62		▭ 62 ▭
63		▭ 63 ▭
64		▭ 64 ▭
65		▭ 65 ▭

SAMPLE

CAMBRIDGE
EXAMINATIONS, CERTIFICATES AND DIPLOMAS
ENGLISH AS A FOREIGN LANGUAGE

University of Cambridge
Local Examinations Syndicate
International Examinations

For Supervisor's use only

Shade here if the candidate is
ABSENT or has WITHDRAWN

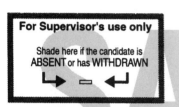

Examination Details	9999/04	99/D99
Examination Title	First Certificate in English	
Centre/Candidate No.	AA999/9999	
Candidate Name	A.N. EXAMPLE	

• Sign here if the details above are correct

• Tell the Supervisor now if the details above
are not correct

Candidate Answer Sheet: FCE Paper 4 Listening

Mark test version below

A	B	C	D	E

Use a pencil

For **Parts 1** and **3**:
Mark ONE letter for
each question.

For example, if you
think **B** is the right
answer to the
question, mark your
answer sheet like this:

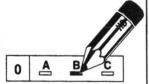

0	A	B	C

For **Parts 2** and **4**:
Write your answers in
the spaces next to the
numbers like this:

0	

Part 1

1	A	B	C
2	A	B	C
3	A	B	C
4	A	B	C
5	A	B	C
6	A	B	C
7	A	B	C
8	A	B	C

Part 2 / Do not write here

9		9
10		10
11		11
12		12
13		13
14		14
15		15
16		16
17		17
18		18

Part 3

19	A	B	C	D	E	F
20	A	B	C	D	E	F
21	A	B	C	D	E	F
22	A	B	C	D	E	F
23	A	B	C	D	E	F

Part 4 / Do not write here

24		24
25		25
26		26
27		27
28		28
29		29
30		30

© UCLES/K & J

124

1

2

3

4

1

2

3

4

1

2

3

4

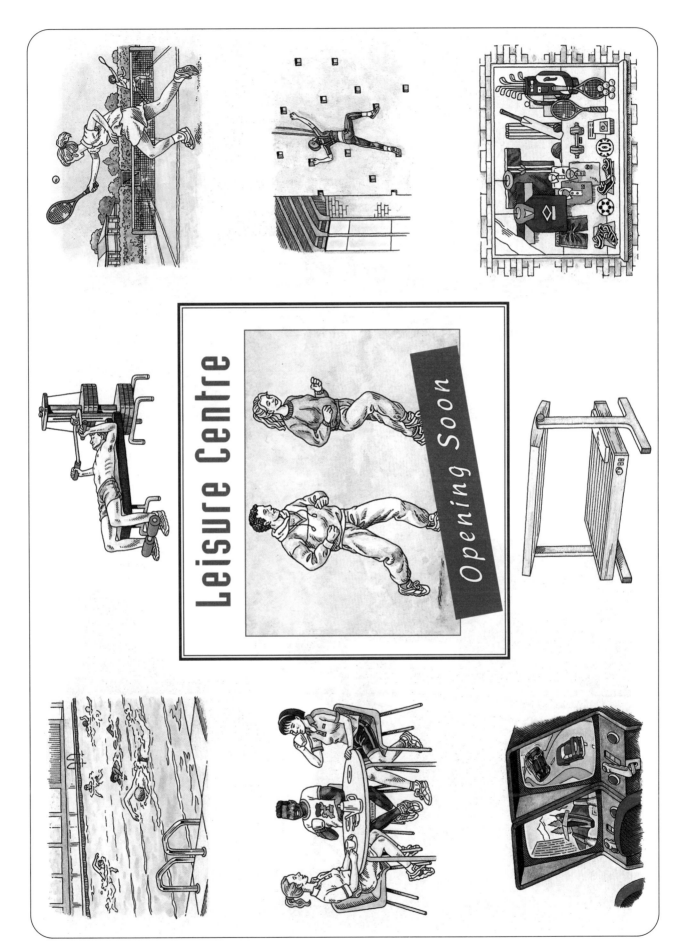

1

2

3

4

1

2

3

4

ADVICE CENTRE